The *Best* • MEMORY MAKERS

SCRAPBOOK LETTERING

50 classic and creative alphabets from the nation's top scrapbook lettering artists

MEMORY
MAKERS
BOOKS

Executive Editor Kerry Arquette   **Founder** Michele Gerbrandt

Associate Editors Kimberly Ball, Shannon Hurd

Senior Editor MaryJo Regier

Art Director Andrea Zocchi

Designer Nick Nyffeler

Production Artist Dawn Knutson

Craft Director Jodi Amidei

Idea Editor Janetta Wieneke

Photographer Ken Trujillo

Contributing Photographers Marc Creedon, Camillo DiLizia, Brenda Martinez

Contributing Writer Anne Wilbur

Editorial Support Dena Twinem

Special Thanks to the Editors of *Memory Makers* magazine

07 06 05 04 03 6 5 4 3 2

Published by Memory Makers Books, an imprint of F & W Publications, Inc.
12365 Huron Street, Suite 500, Denver, CO 80234 Phone 1-800-254-9124 First edition. Printed in China.

Library of Congress Cataloging-in-Publication Data

The best of memory makers scrapbook lettering : 50 classic and creative alphabets from
the nation's top scrapbook lettering artist's.-- 1st ed.
    p. cm.
  Includes index.
  ISBN 1-892127-15-6
  1. Lettering. 2. Scrapbooks. I. Memory Makers Books.

NK3630.3.S37 B47 2003
745.6'1--dc21

2002037981

Distributed to trade and art markets by
F & W Publications, Inc.
4700 East Galbraith Road, Cincinnati, OH 45236
Phone 1-800-289-0963

ISBN 1-892127-15-6

Memory Makers Books is the home of *Memory Makers*, the scrapbook magazine dedicated to educating and inspiring scrapbookers. To subscribe, or for more information, call 1-800-366-6465.
Visit us on the Internet at www.memorymakersmagazine.com

We would like to thank the talented lettering artists whose work has graced the pages of *Memory Makers* magazine throughout the years. We would also like to thank the artists who created beautiful new lettering styles to be introduced for the first time within this book.

Debra Beagle

Debbie Davis

Florence Davis

Cindy Edwards

Sarah Fishburn

Pamela Frye

Erikia Ghumm

Mary Conley Holladay

Lisa Jackson

Pam Klassen

Jan March

Lindsay Ostrum

Allison Pavelek

Michelle Pesce

Narda Poe

Tammy Prueitt

Carol Snyder

Emily Tucker

JoAngela Vassey

Sande Womack

Your talent is an inspiration.

CONTENTS

ntroduction Do you remember when you first learned to write your name in cursive? After much practice, you mastered a new way of connecting letters. Once you grasped the basics, you spent hours doodling your name, experimenting with different ways of writing it. It seemed essential that your signature perfectly convey your style or personality.

By now your signature is so familiar that you can write it without thinking. With a little effort, you can become equally adept at any lettering style in this book. It's not a matter of artistic talent. It's simply a matter of practice.

Why make the effort? Because creative lettering, is the best and least expensive way to unify a scrapbook page design. Your lettered title can make or break a finished page, and your journaling is essential when telling the stories behind the photos. Lettering adds a personal, artistic and homemade touch that is custom-tailored to your page theme and colors.

This book is designed to be used in a number of ways. You may wish to freehand draw the lettering styles seen on these pages. Mastering the technique may take some practice, but will result in a sense of accomplishment and unique titles. You may also choose to photocopy your selected alphabet, enlarging or reducing it as desired. Cut out individual letters and use them to form eye-catching titles. Or trace the letters, using one of the techniques shown on the following pages, onto your paper to create your page title. Cut and adhere them to your scrapbook page.

This book contains 50 different lettering styles. It includes the best alphabets published in *Memory Makers* over the past five years as well as innovative new styles developed by some of the nation's top scrapbook artists. For each lettering style, you'll find a complete set of characters, how-to instructions and scrapbook page illustrations. Use this multitude of design ideas as a starting point for customizing a style to fit your own specific theme or purpose.

Once you discover the creative possibilities, you'll find that the joy of creative lettering is making it truly your own, just like your signature. Happy lettering!

Michele

Michele Gerbrandt
Founding Editor, *Memory Makers*

TOOLS AND SUPPLIES

Practicing the art of creative lettering requires a few essential tools that you may already have on hand.

Pencils

Use a comfortable, easy-to-erase pencil for light tracing and drawing freehand. Choose from standard pencils that can be sharpened or mechanical pencils with lead refills available in different lead weights.

Ruled notebook or graph paper

Keep plenty of ruled notebook or graph paper on hand for practicing different lettering styles, whether tracing or drawing freehand.

Graphing ruler

Use the lines and grid marks of a graphing ruler (see page 9) to help you keep lettering straight and evenly spaced.

Pens and markers

Use archival quality pigment ink pens, which are fade-resistant, waterproof and colorfast. The chart on the right illustrates the variety of pen styles and the results each one creates. A black fine-tip pen is good for journaling and tracing letter outlines. A black bullet-tip pen lets you draw bolder letters and thicker outlines.

Non-abrasive eraser

Non-abrasive erasers safely remove pencil marks without tearing the paper. They are available in different sizes, as well as retractable, pen-styles with refillable eraser sticks.

Paper for title and journaling blocks

Unless you're writing directly on the scrapbook page, you'll need solid-colored, acid-free scrapbook paper on which to pen your lettering for page titles and journaling blocks.

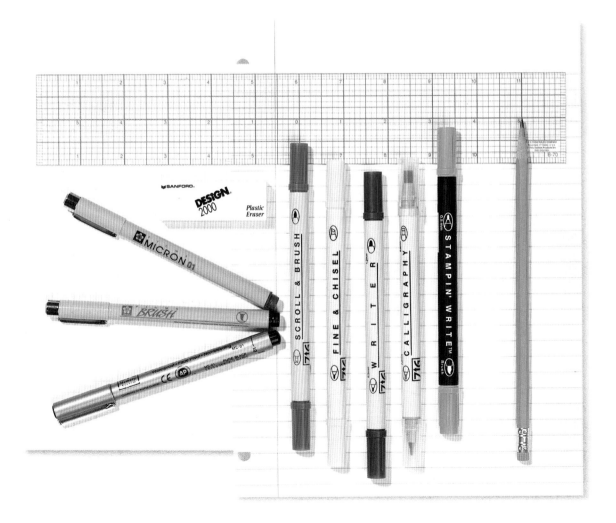

Tools for transferring and tracing lettering

These optional items help make it easier to trace the lettering shown (see page 8 for tips on using these items) in this book and to work with the lettering once it is traced.

- Access to a photocopier for enlarging or reducing letters
- A sunny window or a light box for tracing
- Removable artist's tape to anchor photocopies and paper while tracing
- White typing or copier paper
- Transfer paper
- Translucent paper or vellum
- Embossing stylus
- Scissors, a craft knife and a cutting mat
- Photo-safe adhesives for mounting

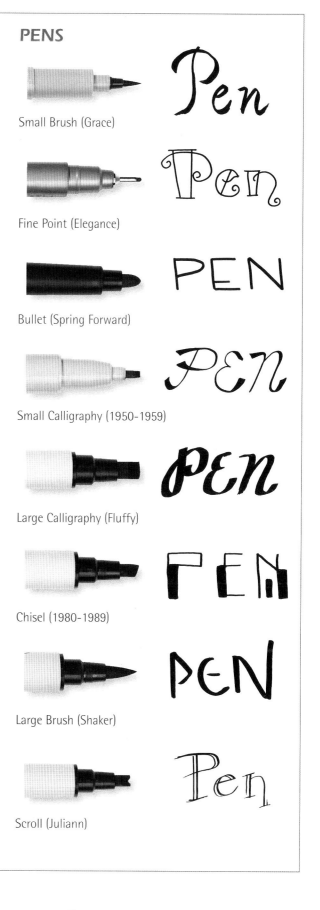

PENS

Small Brush (Grace)

Fine Point (Elegance)

Bullet (Spring Forward)

Small Calligraphy (1950-1959)

Large Calligraphy (Fluffy)

Chisel (1980-1989)

Large Brush (Shaker)

Scroll (Juliann)

METHODS FOR REPRODUCING LETTERING

You can re-create the lettering styles in this book through either tracing or freehand drawing. Tracing letters can help you make beautiful titles and will also help you develop the skills needed to more easily and confidently draw the characters. Several tracing methods are detailed below.

How to trace letters

Before attempting any of the illustrated tracing methods photocopy the alphabet you wish to reproduce, enlarging or reducing it to suit your needs. If the alphabet shown in this book is the perfect size for your project, simply trace it onto white scrap paper. Once you have a complete alphabet on white paper, you're ready to trace the letters to create scrapbook titles.

Light box or sunny window

For light-colored papers, use artist's tape to attach your selected alphabet to a light box, sunny window or an underlit glass table. Lightly pencil guidelines on the paper on which you wish to create your title. Tape this paper atop the alphabet. Trace letters one at a time, in appropriate positions, until your message is complete.

Translucent paper or vellum

Trace any lettering style through translucent paper such as vellum, tracing paper or thin white paper. Lightly pencil guidelines on the paper and lay it over the copy of the selected alphabet. Trace letters one at a time, in appropriate positions, until your message is complete.

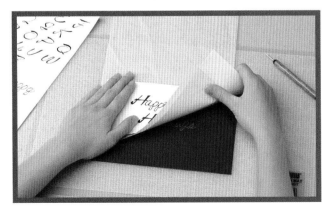

Transfer paper

Use white or yellow transfer paper to trace onto heavy, dark-colored paper. Before transferring lettering, trace it onto scrap paper, using any of the described methods. Place traced lettering atop transfer paper. Layer both sheets of paper (traced and transfer) over a sheet of dark-colored paper. Trace. Use graphite transfer paper for tracing onto light-colored paper.

Embossing stylus

If you don't have transfer paper and want to trace onto dark paper, use an embossing stylus. First trace the lettering onto scrap paper, then place the lettering over dark paper on top of a soft surface such as a cutting mat. When you trace the lettering with an embossing tool, it leaves an indentation that may be traced over with an opaque pen.

How to draw letters freehand

If you are relatively new to freehand lettering, create your title on vellum paper. Place the transparent sheet over lined notebook or graph paper, then follow the underlying grids and lines to maintain consistent letter heights and spacing. Curvy, more arbitrary lettering styles are a good choice for novices because they require less precision and are more forgiving of errors.

Following, are the basic steps for drawing letters freehand. Once you recognize the different components of a lettering style, it becomes much easier to re-create. Drawing letters freehand takes practice, practice, practice!

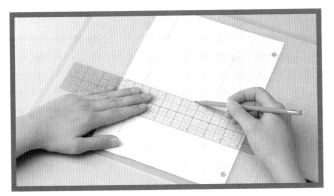

1 Use a ruler to lightly pencil any necessary guidelines, including those for spacing.

2 Sketch the basic shape of each letter without any stroke embellishments.

3 Outline in pencil any wide, thick or fill-in areas as desired.

4 Add any stroke embellishments such as curves, swirls, flowers or other details.

5 Erase and revise as necessary until you're satisfied with each letter.

6 Outline letters with an appropriate pen, then color and embellish if desired (see pages 12-13).

PAGE DESIGN TIPS FOR LETTERING

A great scrapbook page is a work of art. It showcases photos, journaling and embellishments in a way that conveys a message and pleases the eye. Use these tips to help guide you through the process of pulling together your completed page or spread. Remember that a strong scrapbook page is made even more powerful with the appropriate, beautifully lettered title.

2 Match your page theme or style

Choose a lettering style that fits the theme and mood of the page but don't overdo it. Use elaborate letters only for very short titles, or for specific words or letters within a title. Too many elaborate letters draw attention from your photographs. If your page is formal, use a formal lettering style. If your page is whimsical, use a whimsical lettering style.

1 Plan ahead

Determine your page layout and design before you start lettering. Consider photo selection, page theme, paper colors, embellishments and text blocks. Before permanently mounting elements, loosely arrange them on your page. Use scrap paper placeholders for the title and journaling blocks.

3 Determine size, design and placement

If a title is too large, it will overwhelm your layout. If it is too small, it will get lost on your scrapbook page. When designing a title, sketch it in different sizes and styles. Select a title that will work in proportion to the other page elements.

If you have a large space to fill with a short title consider matting the title several times. Or separate the letters that make up the title and mat each individually. String them across the page, inserting small embellishments such as beads, if you wish. If your title is too large for the available space, create it on vellum and mount it so it overlaps other page elements.

4 Disguise your mistakes

We all make mistakes. When it's an "oops" with a permanent pen, you can either live with it (after all, it adds character!), or disguise it. Turn a mistake into a pen stroke embellishment—such as a flower, star or other theme-related doodle—or hide it beneath a theme-related sticker or punched shape.

HOW TO ADD COLOR AND EMBELLISHMENTS

There are dozens of ways to add color and embellishments to your lettering. You can color, shade, paint or chalk lettering. Doodle on it, or in it. Add shadows or enhance finished lettering with stickers, punch art, glitter, stitching. embossing and more. How you add color and embellishments depends upon the lettering style and the look that you wish to achieve. The possibilities are limitless.

Shading with pens and pencils

Black and colored pens generally produce a solid and saturated effect that is great for shading. Simply draw dots, lines or "cross hatches." Use two different colors for a more complex look.

Graduating pencil color

A "fill-in" lettering style has wide open portions that scream to be filled with color and shading. Try graduating the pressure used when applying color to create the illusion that a light source is falling upon the letter. Use less pressure or a blender pencil to soften the transition from dark to light color.

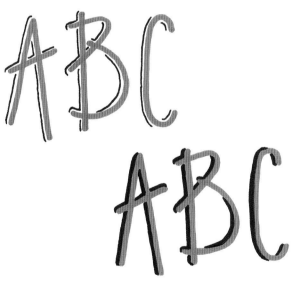

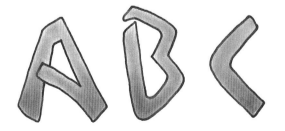

Shadowing

Pencils, chalks and pens are ideal for adding simple shadows to lettering. Simply trace along the edges of your colored lettering. The wider your traced line, the more significant and dramatic the shadow will look.

Shading with chalk

For a subtle look, try adding color with chalk, using a small, sponge-tip applicator for more control. You can shade around each letter as well as color any fill-in areas.

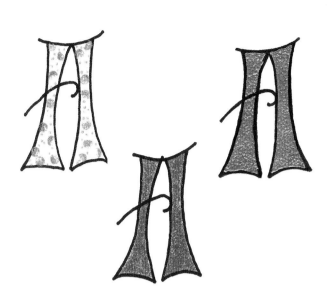

Using stickers, die cuts and punched shapes

Embellishments are the icing on the cake of creative lettering. Stickers, small die cuts and punched shapes are great letter accents, and can also be used to hide pen mistakes.

More colorants to try

Colorants such as stamping inks, embossing inks and powders, glitter and glitter glue can be used to accent lettering.

Freehand or patterned paper "fill"

Create fill patterns by drawing lines, plaids, polka dots or stars. Or use patterned paper to fill in letters.

More embellishments to try

Fabric, embroidery thread, ribbon, fibers, raffia, jute, beads, buttons, sequins, eyelets, wire, brad fasteners, pressed flowers and leaves—virtually any craft supply—can easily be used to enhance your lettering!

A TOUCH OF CLASS

Trends may come and go, but elegance never goes out of style. Like a slender silver candlestick, a flawless black sheath, a gracefully shared compliment, elegance is recognized and appreciated for its classic appeal. A classic lettering style is also universally embraced. Whether it sports sweet little loops, the vulnerable simplistic lines of a child's printing, the confident, smooth curves of a femme fatale or a tailored pinstripe masculine look, you're sure to find a place and a purpose for it within your scrapbook.

BOW TIE

If a scrapbook page is a wrapped present, then this flowing cursive alphabet is the ribbon. You can almost imagine curling different lengths into each casually elegant letter. The widened points even mimic the snipped ends of a pretty bow.

Although it looks fancy, this script is easy to master because it doesn't require perfection. You can replicate the general feel of each letter without having to copy exactly. Starting with penciled guidelines, draw the basic shape of each letter. Connect letters if it seems natural, such as the letter m flowing into the letter a. If the connection seems awkward, as in the letter w followed by the letter e, just end the first letter and start the next one beside it.

When you're happy with the overall flow of each word, add extra swirls and curves where needed. The transitions from thin lines to thick are an important element in this lettering, so be sure to outline the thicker parts of each letter. Note that all lines in this alphabet are curved except for the widened letter ends, which are blunt.

Now it's time to color. Dress up this style with a metallic pen on dark paper, or go more casual with bright colors. Add fancy embellishments or let the letters stand alone. Whatever your preference, this beautiful script is versatile enough for almost any purpose.

FLUFFY

Write the alphabet using your fanciest printing. Then write it again with your best cursive. Now choose the characters from each set that you like the best. What do you get? The handwriting you've always wanted—a sophisticated cross between fancy printed and cursive characters.

This lettering requires consistent heights and even lines, so be sure to pencil guidelines before you start. After lightly drawing each letter, decide whether you want any characters to be connected as in a cursive style. Then draw the connecting lines. When you're satisfied, trace each letter with a medium to thick pen. The pen tip should be uniform because the lines in each character are the same width and don't vary.

To fully master this style takes some practice. Start out by tracing it several times on inexpensive ruled notebook paper. Once you get the feel for each character, try drawing words freehand. You'll be glad you invested the time because Fluffy is a terrific look to add to your repertoire of lettering styles for both captions and titles.

ABCDEFG
HIJKLM
NOPQRST
UVWXYZ

abcdefghi
jklmnopqr
stuvwxyz
1234567890

Debbie and Sande
BEST FRIENDS

·My Best Friend·
we share many things
there is lots of laughter
and sometimes tears
as our days together
turn into years.

VARIATIONS

Reminiscent of old-fashioned cursive typewriters, Fluffy lettering is ideal for formal or heritage themes. When using this style exclusively, write the more significant title words with a heavier weight pen to make them stand out. For a less formal look, use Fluffy for the title alone and write the captions in a more casual style. Because this lettering is simple and uncluttered, you can match the letter colors to your page without compromising impact.

mom and Perry Como

Now—More Dates—More Fun!

In the winter of 1946, my mom, Barbra Whittemore, won a contest after participating in the DuBarry Success Course. She won a brand new wardrobe and a trip to New York to do some modeling and to meet Perry Como. She also appeared in the February 10, 1947 issue of Life Magazine.

ELEMENTARY

Do you remember learning to print? Lips pressed together in concentration, eyes focused on blue rule lines and a small fist squeezing a freshly sharpened #2 pencil, you carefully tried to copy perfectly printed letters. The result was always less than perfect but reflected your individuality. Elementary lettering captures this charming personality.

Unlike grade-school printing, this style is deliberately imperfect. The letters only loosely follow guidelines. Vertical and diagonal lines start and stop at different heights, avoiding that too-straight look. Not all loops are closed, as in the letters B and O, suggesting that the characters were written quickly. And just to add to the cuteness, the letters g and y have sweet little loops.

You really can't make a mistake with this style if you're able to leave your perfectionist tendencies behind. Draw guidelines only if you want the letters to casually line up. Then pencil each character and trace with the pen color and thickness of your choice.

Use this lettering as a starting point for creating your own personal style of printing. Customize each letter with little idiosyncrasies that make it your own. The greater the imperfection, the greater the charm!

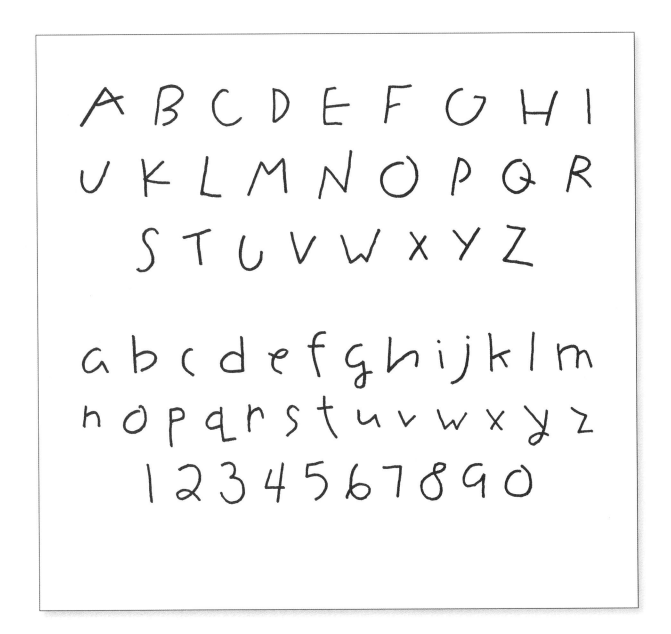

The fifth grade students of Stony Creek Elementary ran a city for a day... they made the laws and elected a mayor and a towne sheriff. Dillon was chosen to be the manager accountant of the television station.

November 2-0-0-1 5th Grade

Young Ameritowne

NEWS 4

NEWS 4 Colorado's News Channel

VARIATIONS

Elementary lettering is simple enough for captions as well as titles. Because it's quick and easy to write, you have more time to get creative. Decorate characters with themed stickers, punched shapes and other embellishments. For added whimsy, replace an entire letter with a graphic element, such as a soccer ball for the letter O.

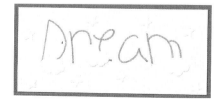

SIGNATURE

It's the contemporary yet classic cursive handwriting you've always dreamed of. Confident lines, smooth curves, simple flourishes. Before you say, "I can't write like that," give it a try. With some lined paper and a little practice, you'll soon be the envy of your scrapbooking friends.

To get the feel of each letter, lay ruled notebook paper over a photocopy of the letters and trace each character. Use the lines as a guide to keep the letters a consistent height. Draw each letter until you feel comfortable with its shape. You may notice that this style draws its contemporary as well as classic feel from the combination of mostly printed uppercase letters with cursive lowercase letters.

Now practice words and phrases, starting with your name and short titles. Note that while the uppercase letters are often unconnected, the lowercase letters are usually joined, whether directly or by gently touching edges. Lowercase letters may be unconnected when the first letter ends low and the second letter starts high, as in the word "an." Rather than relying on rigid rules to determine which letters should connect, focus on the overall visual flow, striving for movement throughout the word.

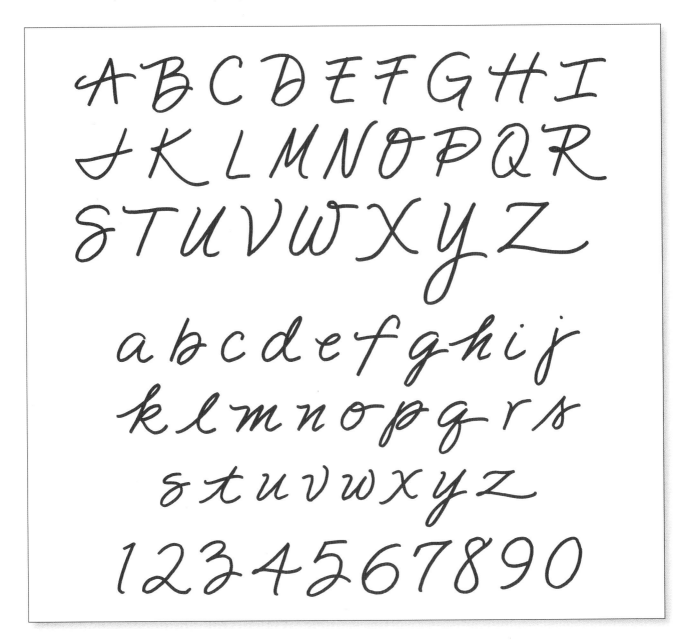

VARIATIONS

In Signature's uppercase letters, most of the horizontal lines cross over the verticals. This detail gives the style a feeling of movement. To further accentuate this sensation, embellish the title with a thin shadow line and freeform swirled lines as seen in the *Falling for Fall* page at the right. You can almost sense the breeze moving over the page.

PINSTRIPE

Who says that pinstripes are just for men's fashion? They perfectly "suit" these contemporary, masculine letters, resulting in a tailored style that emphasizes vertical lines.

Start with guidelines to keep your letter heights even. Then pencil the basic letter shapes with single lines. Outline the wider parts of each character by drawing additional lines on either side of your base lines. If the line is straight, then the outlines should be straight and squared off at the top, as in the letter H. If the line curves, then the outlines should narrow and blend into the curve as it turns horizontal, as in the letter C. When a letter does not have a vertical line, such as the letter X, then widen one diagonal line and leave the other line single. Note how the inside lines became the pinstripes!

A few sketching notes: Most of the uppercase characters are the same height except Y, which drops down below the baseline. Also, for variety, the lowercase g and j drop down lower than p and q.

The fun part is deciding how to colorize your letters. Consider black outlines and colored pinstripes, leaving the fill-in areas empty. Or draw all lines black and color the fill-in areas. Whatever you choose, you'll like the clean, crisp look of a well-tailored suit.

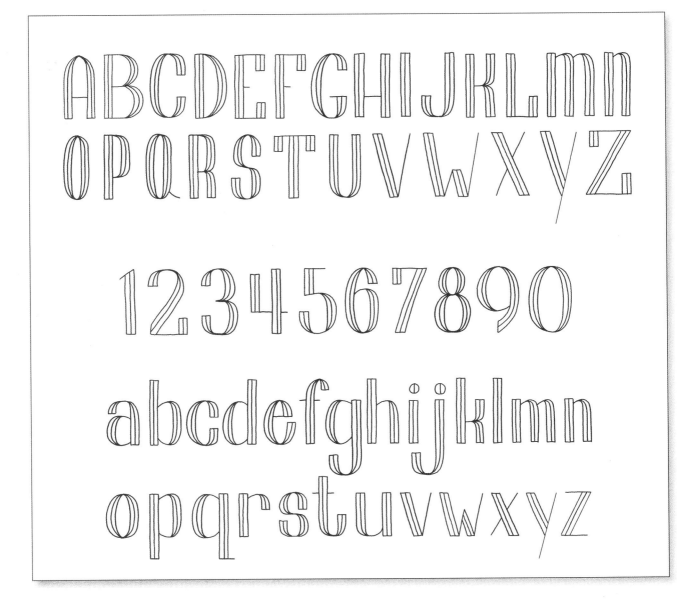

VARIATIONS

Pinstripe lettering offers multiple design options. For a more translucent quality, color the pinstripes while leaving the letter outlines black. To give the characters more weight, color each stripe, adding horizontal lines to change colors within each stripe. For a bold graphic element, use a single Pinstripe character as the first letter of a title or caption.

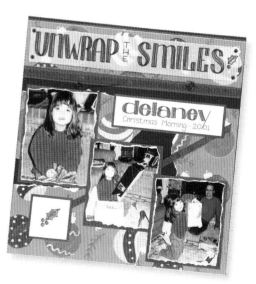

SAMPLER

The needle arts provide a wealth of ideas for creative scrapbookers. Quilting, appliqué and cross-stitch patterns, among others, can be easily adapted for scrapbook designs. The same holds true for needlepoint alphabets. This traditional lettering, inspired by the look of hand-stitched letters, yields the same effect without a needle and thread.

When arranging these letters, it's helpful to use graph paper as a grid, similar to a cross-stitch pattern. You can pencil a grid directly on paper or place graph paper on a light box so the grid shows through. The grid ensures uniform letter heights and spacing and makes it easy to draw diagonals. To determine the size of the grid, decide how wide you want the thicker parts of each letter. Make the grid the same size. If, for example, you want the line width to be ¼", use a ¼" grid.

Begin by outlining the thickest part of each letter. Then draw the thin lines, ending with the curved embellishments. Note that the thin lines may be straight and diagonal, as in the letter M, or more curved, as in the letter A.

When you're satisfied with the letters, color the outlines and fill with either a matching or contrasting color. Although this lettering style has a traditional look, you don't have to use conventional scrapbook supplies to create it. How about fabric and embroidery floss?

VARIATIONS

Sampler letters provide an uncluttered, old-fashioned look when simply penned in a solid color. Machine-sewn borders and frames tie in the stitched theme. For an even more homespun look, fabricate the letters from embroidery floss and bits of calico, gingham and denim.

SHAKER

Sometimes your lettering just needs some space. Space to make a statement, stretch out and relax. Shaker does just that, and then some. It's casually sophisticated, elegantly whimsical and quietly bold.

Creating Shaker can take no time at all, which means you can quickly move on to the fun part—filling in all those letters. Spread out your supplies because there's lots of room for variation. You'll find many uses for this versatile style that works for most contemporary themes. Just give it some space!

Like the famous Shaker style, less is more, so be selective when choosing words to feature using this style. If you want the letters to roughly line up, pencil guidelines. Then sketch the basic shape of each character with a single line. Leave adequate space between letters. Now outline the letters so they are transformed into block-style characters.

The exaggerated widths of letters such as h, m and n are a key element of this style, so be sure to stretch them out. Note that most of the letter loops are wide open, especially in the letters a, b and g and that the middle line in the letters E and F are not connected to the rest of the character.

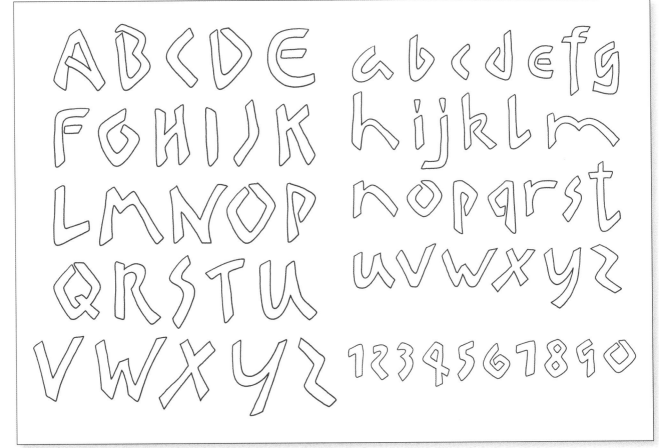

VARIATIONS

Shaker letters are quick and easy to outline, so you have plenty of time to get creative with color. Try painting polka dot and plaid designs with colored pens. Integrate the outlines into a graphic element such as a blazing sun, and color everything shades of yellow and orange. Or simply cut each letter from softly patterned paper.

SLANT

Here's a fast lettering lesson. Start with a basic printed alphabet. Drop the lowercase f and s and every uppercase letter slightly below the baseline. Slant all horizontal lines and have them cross over the verticals. Leave the loops open. Now you have Slant, a tall, narrow style that allows you to fit a lot of words in a small space.

Of course there are more nuances to this lettering, but Slant teaches a valuable lesson: By changing a few details of an alphabet, you can come up with your own personalized lettering. All it takes is a little experimentation.

To re-create this lettering, start with guidelines to keep things generally straight. Pencil each character and finish with the pen color of your choice.

Notice that this style is meant to look like handwriting, so the lettering is not precise. Vertical lines in letters such as H and N are different heights. The crossovers extend beyond the vertical lines, like a quick scrawl. And the letters a, b, d and p are not perfectly joined, which adds to its casual feeling.

Aa Bb Cc Dd Ee Ff Gg
Hh Ii Jj Kk Ll Mm Nn
Oo Pp Qq Rr Ss Tt Uu Vv
Ww Xx Yy Zz
1234567890

Christmastime

It's amazing how the cuzzies have grown when you add kids and husbands! Too bad Steve had to leave early.

The brothers and Steve relax after a wonderful Christmas dinner.

VARIATIONS

Slant works equally well for both titles and captions. The letters are even simple enough to re-create with craft wire. In the *My Girls* page, both the white craft wire and small seed beads are held in place by white sewing thread. The center border design adds further embellishment with gray metal shapes and buttons attached with embroidery floss.

My Girls

I think I might be the luckiest mom around to be able to call two of the sweetest little girls I know my daughters.

The top reasons I know my girls love each other.

♥ Whenever Brinley cries, Alexa runs to get her baby doll and silky blanket for her

♥ Whenever Alexa cries, Brinley pat's her back

♥ When Alexa sits on the couch to watch cartoons Brinley wants to sit right next to her

♥ Brinley SQUEALS with delight whenever Alexa runs around

♥ Alexa tells Brinley, "It's OK baby you be alright"

♥ When Brinley needs her diaper changed Alexa brings down a clean diaper without even being asked

ALL FOR ONE

If you disliked grade-school grammar, here's your chance to break all the rules. Begin a sentence with a lower-case letter. Don't capitalize a proper noun. Even put uppercase letters in the middle of words. Shocking! And delightful.

If you can draw two parallel lines, you can write All for One lettering. Just choose a letter height, draw two lines that distance apart, and pencil the characters between the lines. The greater the distance between your guidelines, the taller the letters appear.

Keep the letters as straight as possible. Emphasize the exaggerated elements such as the small half circle in the letter e and the tall ovals in the letters a, b and d. Variety is created by charming inconsistencies. For example, some curves, such as in the letters a and e and the number 6, are completed, while other curves in letters like g, j, s and t seem to stop short before they've completed the turn.

The best thing about All for One is its simplified approach. You only need one set of characters to convey the message, so why mess with upper- and lowercase? Just don't tell your English teacher.

abcdefghijkLM
nopqrstuvwxyz
1234567890

VARIATIONS

All for One is an easygoing linear style that looks good in any size, large or small. When using this lettering for a title and caption on the same page, add emphasis to the larger letters by drawing them with a thick pen and outlining them with a dark color.

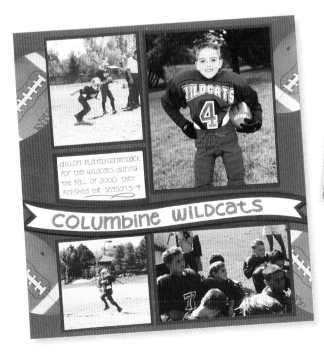

CONTEMPO

Ever spin a yarn, tell a tall tale or stretch the truth? As this lettering style illustrates, exaggeration can be an art. Stretching letter widths and vertical lines creates a classic, elegant look, and the lowercase letters provide a sophisticated understatement. With a few embellishments, however, this style easily adapts to a more whimsical theme.

This lettering can be easily mastered by practicing with a calligraphy pen. To keep the letters a consistent height, first lightly pencil guidelines. Holding the pen tip at a 45-degree angle, draw the lines of each letter using separate strokes.

For example, for the letter b, first draw the tall vertical line from the top to the bottom. Lift the pen from the paper and place the tip slightly up from the bottom. To complete the letter, draw the oval in a clockwise direction until it meets the bottom of the first stroke.

In general, draw the vertical lines from top to bottom, the curved lines from left to right and the round parts in a clockwise direction. Pay attention to exaggerating the widths of the letters h, m, n, s, u, v, w and x to capture the look of this alphabet. This style works particularly well when lettered along an arc or a curve. Simply use a journaling template to draw guidelines.

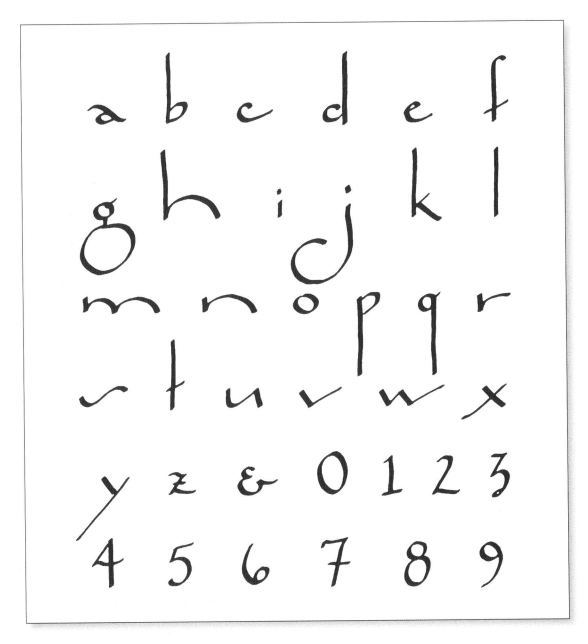

carole & harrison dewegeli
dec. 20, 1958

to have and
to hold,
from this
day forward

abcdef
ghijkl
mnopqr
stuvwx
yz

VARIATIONS

To convert the classic look of Contempo to a fun and whimsical theme, simply doodle small embellishments with a fine-tip pen. Try squiggles, swirls, stars, zigzags, sun rays, circles, squares, dots and dashes. Use these samples as a starting point for your own unique embellishments.

a work of heart

ELEGANCE

They say that opposites attract. Perhaps that's why the straight, asymmetrical fill-in areas of Elegance pair so well with its thin and curly lines. It's the contrast that appeals, like black and white, smooth and bumpy, sweet and salty.

If you think of Elegance as two distinct or opposite parts, it's much easier to create. In most cases you start with the fill-in area and then draw the curly lines. However, for round letters like C, G and O, and numbers such as 3, 6 and 9, draw the curved lines first and then the straight line for the fill-in space. The number 8 is simply one big double swirl.

Use penciled guidelines for both upper- and lowercase letters. For each columnar fill-in space, pencil-draw two straight and slanted lines, using a ruler as necessary. Close off the space with two horizontal lines that extend beyond the corners. Note that these asymmetrical areas taper up or down depending upon the letter. Complete each letter by drawing the thin curly lines.

Trace each penciled letter with a dark pen and color the fill-in areas as desired. Your page theme might suggest a coloring scheme or a variation for the swirls. Consider decorating with contrasting colors, patterns and textures.

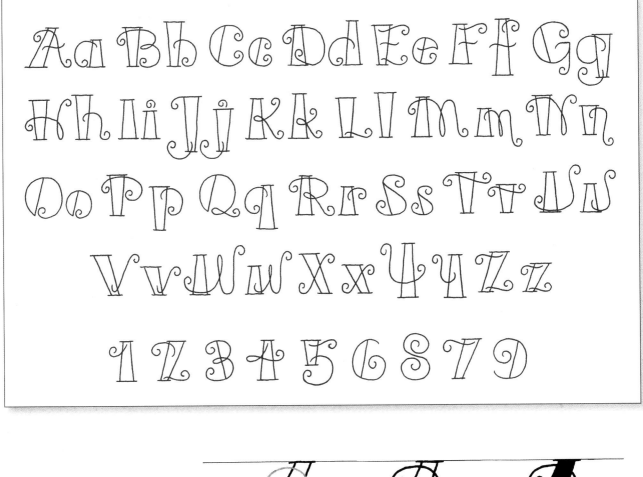

VARIATIONS

The individual boxes on the *Spring* page mimic the shapes of the letters' fill-in areas. Strung on a length of red craft wire with swirled ends, the curved design adds a touch of whimsy. For variety, transform the curls at the ends of each letter into other shapes such as leaves, teardrops, flowers, balloons, knots, stars or whatever fits the theme.

WHIMSICAL BLOCK

There's nothing symmetrical about this alphabet. The characters are different heights. The lines in each character are different lengths. In fact, this lettering is perfectly imperfect. But that's what gives it personality and gives you freedom to make mistakes. You can goof and nobody will notice. In fact, the more you tilt and slant, the better the look.

You can trace these block letters or easily draw them free-hand. Using a pencil, draw each letter with single lines, varying the tops and bottoms so nothing appears to line up.

Leave adequate space between each character. Next, outline each letter, adding rectangular shapes at the ends of each line. When you are satisfied, trace each letter outline with a thin dark pen.

Perfect for contemporary photos or any page with a light-hearted theme, block letters like Whimsical Block beg for color, whether saturated hues from colored pens or the soft shades of colored pencils and watercolors. Experiment with different blending and shading techniques. If you make a mistake, no one will be the wiser, because it's supposed to be imperfect!

VARIATIONS

One way to tie a title to a page theme is to add graphic elements to the title that reflect the action in the photos, such as the acorns in *Nuts Over Acorns* and the waves in *Jet Skiing Fun*. To add even more whimsy, embellish with dimensional items such as wire, beads and stars.

JULIANN

If you've ever tied a locket of baby hair in a pretty ribbon and safely encapsulated it on a baby page, you'll instantly recognize the inspiration for this lettering. As wispy as those soft, strawberry blonde curls, Juliann letters almost look like they could be formed from individual strands.

Juliann has a casual, sketchy look that is designed to look imperfect. So your only challenge is to emulate the free-form style, not copy it exactly. Start with guidelines if you want the letters to loosely line up. Then sketch each letter, adding short crossbars and double lines where necessary. Notice that few of the lines meet; they either cross over or don't touch at all.

Trace the penciled letters with the pen color of choice and add color between the double lines if desired. You can get creative with the materials you use to create Juliann lettering, but make sure the locks continue to look light and feathery as infant curls!

VARIATIONS

Whether it's a sophisticated graduation page or a delightful page featuring a child's "first," Juliann lettering adds just the right touch. Coloring this style can be as easy as smudging chalk around a title, embellishing with colored pens or adding free-form strokes with a watercolor brush.

CHARITY BALL

Dress it up. Dress it down. Fill it in. Leave it empty. With its clean lines and gentle swirls, Charity Ball is versatile enough to adapt to a variety of page themes.

The consistent heights and straight fill-in areas of this style make guidelines a necessity. Start by sketching each character with single lines. Note that the lowercase letters are extra tall, which gives the entire style a feeling of height. Also, some uppercase letters like A, B, D, R and S drop below the baseline, almost like dropped capitals.

To create the fill-in areas, simply draw one or two lines following the initial lettering guidelines. You might prefer to use a ruler for this portion. Notice that each fill-in space is slightly tilted to the right. Look at the letter A, for example. If you connected the top left corner to the bottom right corner of the fill-in area, you'd end up with a straight line. This image may help you determine how steeply to slant each letter.

When you're happy with the sketched characters, trace them with a dark pen. Then color the fill-in areas, adorn them with texture and pattern, or simply leave them blank. Charity Ball works just about any way you design it.

the many
FACES
of
TIGGER

For all her attitude and orner-
iness, Tigger is quite the pretty,
photogenic girl! For whatever
reason she's also finally mel-
lowing out around Tim. She'll
even climb up on him for pets.

VARIATIONS

Charity Ball's clean lines and pretty swirls call for simple
embellishment. You might opt to leave the fill-in spaces
empty or just fill them with a single color. Add texture with
an easy pattern such as a wavy line. As illustrated in *Auntie's
Shower*, apply glitter over colored pencil for added sparkle.

The
Aunties Shower
My mother threw me a beautiful dessert shower
at her house on friday night. I helped her make
the desserts that day, and Dad's beautiful flowers were
the perfect decoration. All the women "aunties" were
there and the baby and I felt truly celebrated!

I Believe...

FALL
FUN

ARCHITECTURE

Those domestic goddesses who've had their share of laundry disasters know that the only way to salvage a favorite yet shrunken sweater is to dampen it and play tug-of-war with the now preemie-sized sleeves. Imagine doing the same with a basic uppercase alphabet and you've created Architecture lettering.

Every letter is expanded horizontally as if someone tugged and stretched each character as wide as it could go. For added flair, the S is stretched vertically. Because of its simplicity, this style works as well for captions as it does for titles. Its lack of embellishment also makes it a good choice for fast pages and masculine themes.

With the exception of the letter S, Architecture's uppercase letters fit between two parallel guidelines. Just determine the letter height and draw each character with exaggerated widths and angles. Note how the diagonal lines are stretched out in letters such as N and Y. The horizontal lines in the letters A, E and H are also lowered almost as far as possible.

To keep the letter widths consistent, try to match each width to the almost triangular letter A. Think about stretching that tiny sweater and you're on the right track.

VARIATIONS

Quickly enhance Architecture's horizontal, masculine style with a variety of shadowing techniques. Shadow thick letters with a thin black pen, or reverse the idea and draw thin black letters shadowed by a thick colored pen. Embellish with random dot clusters, sophisticated stickers or even a banner-flying airplane.

SIMPLE STRETCH

Remember the popular childhood game Pick-Up Stix? You'd drop a wad of what looked like giant colored toothpicks on the floor, creating a random design. If that design actually formulated into letters of the alphabet, you'd see something that looked an awful lot like Simple Stretch.

The key to this alphabet is that each character is drawn with separate lines that cross each other at junctions. For example, the letter A is composed of three straight lines and three crossovers. The letter B includes one straight line, two curved lines and four crossovers. Notice that letters such as J and Y droop down noticeably below your baseline. The beauty of these characters is that the more crooked they are, the better they look.

If you focus on each line or curve rather than each letter, re-creating this style is a cinch. Just pencil in each letter and trace with black pen. Because it is not overly embellished, Simple Stretch works for both journaling and titles. Use this style alone for a simple, childlike effect, or dress it up with added decorations, like Easter eggs in the corner of each letter, to create something decidedly more festive.

VARIATIONS

Try shadowing Simple Stretch characters with light gray or a lighter shade of the letter color. For added dimension, draw each letter on a separate square and pop every other letter off the page with self-adhesive foam spacers. Combine Simple Stretch with letters in a different style, coloring the alternative letters and setting them against a pastel background, while writing the Simple Stretch-lettered words in plain black ink.

CURVED CLASSIC

Look closely. You won't find a single straight line. Although it seems too fancy to be easy, this lettering style is surprisingly simple because there's no perfect version of each letter. Nothing needs to be straight with this romantic, curvy style.

If you want the letters to generally line up, start with some guidelines. First lightly sketch or trace each letter with a pencil. Remember, all the lines are curved, so draw with a relaxed, loose hand.

Next, draw over the letter outlines with a thin dark pen. Color the fill-in parts of each letter with markers, pencils, watercolors, chalk or other supplies.

This style works well with a variety of themes from classic heritage to toddler antics. Keep the letters upright, or tilt them for fun and flair. Design the fill-in colors, patterns or textures to suit your page. Accent with decorative embellishments such as quilling, wire and beads. However you create these curvy characters, you'll enjoy the freedom from sticking to the straight and narrow.

Mi Abuela

Cuba

1909-1981

When I was a little girl, my favorite place to be was with my Abuela. My Abuela & my mother came to the U.S. from Cuba in 1963. After I was born, my Abuela lived with us for many years. When I was little I had a hard time saying Abuela & nicknamed her Bodi (short for Abuela). Bodi taught me to speak Spanish & was always giving me hugs & kisses, & singing to me. I love this picture of my Abuela. She was about 18 (circa 1927). I can see myself in her. I have her eyes, mouth, and nose. She was truly a wonderful woman and I miss my Abuela very much.

Catalina Amandi

Reading Rocks
and so does crawling

VARIATIONS

Curved Classic letters look terrific when shaded with colored pencils. For added dimension, shade the lettering background with colored chalk and gold leaf the fill-in spaces. Accentuate the letter curves by bending and beading craft-wire embellishments.

GRACE

"Seemingly effortless beauty or charm of movement, form or proportion." There you have it—a definition of the word, "grace." It certainly applies to this lovely manuscript writing. The gentle curves and flowing lines of Grace lettering are equally appropriate for both titles and captions.

Mastering this style takes practice, but is well worth it. Begin by tracing the alphabet and numbers repeatedly on ruled notebook paper. Use the lines as a guide to keep the letters a consistent height. Notice how lowercase letters such as b, d and h are actually taller than the uppercase characters. The uppercase letters N, V, W and X have matching tall flourishes.

When you feel confident enough to create your own titles and captions, begin writing on penciled guidelines. Draw each character, revising as necessary. When finished, trace over the letters with a pen. The pen tip should be uniform because the lines in each character do not vary in width.

You'll find Grace an appealing style for any theme or time period. Its classic, handwritten look gives the impression that the words were worth the time it took to scribe them beautifully...gracefully.

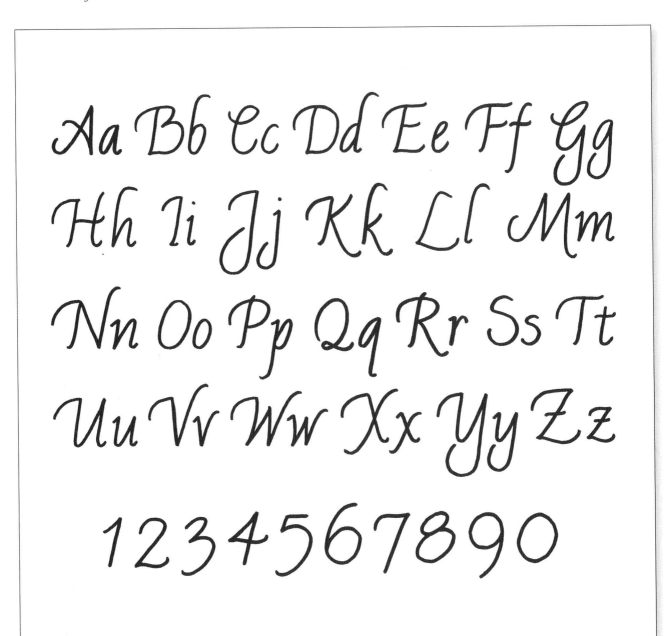

VARIATIONS

Tired of the same old adhesive? *Dunsmuir House* illustrates the use of brass brads holding vellum titles in place. Another idea: Tie together two phrases by slipping craft wire through metal eyelets and twisting into a curly bow. Want a more floral look? Embellish any lettering with tiny punched leaves.

The embossed title above takes lettering to new "heights." To re-create, use a stylus to emboss the copper from the back side, writing each letter backwards. Hold the copper piece with kitchen tongs over a gas stove or candle to discolor it. When it's cool, trim around the title. Punch a square and a small hole to attach the heart charm. Write the remaining words on metallic gold vellum and tear edges. Attach the vellum with copper-embossed brass brads.

PUTTIN' ON THE RITZ

"High hats and narrow collars, white spats and lots of dollars." Irving Berlin's lyrics perfectly describe these tall, narrow letters with their elegant style and cool sophistication. These particular characters must be puttin' on airs, however, because they can dress down as easily as they can dress up.

Puttin' on the Ritz is easy to reproduce as long as you use a ruler and guidelines to keep the letters the same height and each character standing straight and tall. Start by penciling each character with a single line. Notice that horizontal lines are either "shoulder" high, as in the letters E, F and H, or "knee" low, as in the letters A and G. The lowercase t is also exaggerated in height.

Once you've sketched each letter, draw the outlines, taking care to keep the letter widths consistent. Use a ruler, as necessary, to keep the lines straight. Then trace and color each letter.

Puttin' on the Ritz is especially well-suited for cutting letters from solid or patterned paper. The lack of detail makes the cutting go faster, and the paper choice determines whether you end up with a simple, uncluttered caption or a fancy, sophisticated title. For extra glitz, outline each patterned letter with gold pen or sprinkle with glitter. A la Berlin, "you'll declare it's simply topping."

VARIATIONS

A streamlined style reminiscent of the Art Deco era, Puttin' on the Ritz is appropriate for a variety of occasions, from casual bathtime fun to elegant vintage portraits. If you can't get enough color and pattern, cut the letter shapes out of printed vellum and layer patterned paper beneath the letter openings. As illustrated in *Happy New Year*, the result is amazingly sophisticated.

FUN & FUNKY

RYAN, RYAN, ISAIAH, AUSTIN, MARSHALL AND JOSH.

Boy Scout Party

HO HO HO

RYAN

JOSH AND MARSHALL

WE PLAYED A FUN GAME AT THE SCOUT CHRISTMAS PARTY! EACH BOY HAD TO ANSWER A CHRISTMAS TRIVIA QUESTION. IF THEY GOT IT RIGHT, THEY ROLLED THE DICE, AND GOT THE SAME NUMBER OF COTTON BALLS. THEY DIPPED THE COTTON BALLS IN LOTION TO MAKE A SANTA BEARD. THE SCOUT WITH THE FULLEST BEARD WON!

ISAIAH

Creative, entertaining and simply oozing with personality, these center-stage lettering styles are distinct enough to share the spotlight with your most vibrant photos. Each alphabet has been designed to add that certain "je ne sais quoi" to your scrapbook page, not only supporting, but also carrying forward, your page theme. Whether bursting with sunflowers, decked out with holly leaves, mimicking Roman columns or emulating cross-stitch, all these alphabets are compellingly unique. Add your own embellished or drawn modifications, and most of these alphabets can be used on a variety of pages. Draw ideas from our variations or let your imagination run free and applaud as your titles steal the show.

HOLLY

Just try not to hum "Deck the halls with boughs of holly" as you decorate these letters with handmade holly boughs. These simple printed characters entwined with festive garlands are sure to put you in the holiday spirit, whether it's July or December.

Start by penciling each character using guidelines if desired. Then decide which characters to decorate. Follow the lettering guide to pencil swirling lines around each letter.

If desired, extend a long swirling line behind a group of unadorned letters, as shown on the facing page. When you're satisfied with the placement of the lines, pencil in the holly leaves and berries.

Now pull out your box of colored pens, because using different pen tips really adds to the look of this lettering. Outline the leaves and berries and color the swirling lines with a thin pen. Use a thicker point to draw the letters, highlighting with a thin black pen if desired. Finally, color in the leaves and berries. Now your letters are officially "decked."

CROSS STITCH

If you've ever tried your hand at counted cross-stitch, you'll recognize the inspiration for these handmade letters. The building blocks for each character are tiny squares that mimic the X-shaped stitches of the popular craft. Stacked vertically or horizontally, the squares form straight lines. Arranged diagonally, the squares touch corner to corner to form rough diagonals.

The easiest way to re-create this style is with graph paper or a checkerboard grid drawn with a ruler and pencil. When using graph paper, make sure the grid is the appropriate size. You can reduce or enlarge it using a photocopy machine. Lay a sheet of vellum or tracing paper over the sized grid so the lines show through. Then fill in the appropriate squares for each letter. If you happen to have some cross-stitch patterns for inspiration, try designing embellishments using the same tiny squares in various colors.

As seen on the page below, you can add a touch of whimsy by slightly tilting the grid for each character. This style is perfect for adding a homemade touch to any page, especially those quilt-style layouts. Refer to *Memory Makers Quilted Scrapbooks* for gobs of inspiration but, beware, you might get bit by the quilting bee.

Babies dream of clean diapers, warm milk, snuggling close to Mom and soft kisses from a two-year-old sister. Mothers dream for their daughters to grow happy healthy and strong, to follow their hearts, remember who they are and expect to be treated like a Queen. Our Heavenly Father dreams for his children to Return with Honor.

Aa Bb Cc Dd Ee Ff Gg
Hh Ii Jj Kk Ll Mm Nn
Oo Pp Qq Rr Ss Tt Uu
Vv Ww Xx Yy Zz

FRIENDSHIP

FRIENDSHIP

VARIATIONS

If you're more of a seamstress than a cross-stitch enthusiast, create titles using a variety of decorative sewing techniques. Add pen stroke dash and dot "stitched" lines to handwritten, sticker or template letters. Create "fabric" letters by penciling in swirls, stars and other shapes. Tear or overlay paper pieces to make homey quilted letters and warm and friendly titles.

LOVE

PATCHWORK

QUILT

HEARTS ENTWINED

Hearts for love, holly for Christmas, apples for school days, flowers for spring, snowflakes for winter. Whatever the theme, you can always create a matching design. Apply the idea to lettering and the result is this elegant, versatile style.

The Hearts Entwined concept is simple. Start with basic lettering and add themed doodles. These letters are fancy enough to use in separate letter boxes or as the featured first letter of a word or journaling paragraph.

When drawing or tracing these letters, start with guidelines to keep everything straight. Draw each character with single lines. Then go back and widen the thicker vertical parts. Once you're satisfied with the basic letters, draw over them with a dark pen, adding small triangles, or serifs, at the ends of each line.

For the doodled embellishments, pick up your pencil again. Combine swirls and dots with hearts, apples, holly leaves, snowflakes, flowers or whatever fits your theme. Color over the thin lines with a dark pen and fill in the other shapes as desired.

VARIATIONS

Hearts Entwined lettering can be easily adapted to fit any theme. Draw your inspiration from symbols associated with the events featured on your scrapbook pages. Wrap your title letters in decorative vines, allow the embellishment to sprout, twine and fill up the hollows within the letters.

SPRING

SCHOOL

RECITAL

SUNBURST

"You are my sunshine, my only sunshine, you make me happy when skies are gray." You might be humming this familiar song as you outline the triangular rays of these sunny letters. Perfect for the little sunshines in your life, a bright day in May or a hot afternoon at the beach, Sunburst literally glows with warmth and energy.

Don't bother with guidelines because these letters are designed to go up and down so that you can nestle each letter next to the previous. Just pencil the basic shape of each letter with single lines including the small crossbars, or serifs. Almost every letter has a little swirl to represent the sun, although you don't have to draw sun rays on each letter. Note that in the lowercase alphabet, the vertical lines stretch extra high and low, as in the letters h, l, g and j.

When you're satisfied with the letter placements and shapes, draw the outlines to create fill-in characters. Add little triangles around the swirls and an extra dot or swirled shape inside. Trace each letter outline with dark pen and color in. Then brighten each sunburst with vivid yellow, glowing orange, fiery red or any hot colors from your arsenal.

VARIATIONS

Sunburst is a whimsical lettering style designed for pages featuring upbeat events. You can vary the look by changing the graphic element. For example, *Lake Mead* depicts a hot day at the lake with squiggly orange heat waves emanating from each letter. The feeling is further emphasized by blending orange and yellow pencils when coloring in each letter.

SUMMERTIME FUN! JUNE 1998 AT HERITAGE SQUARE NEAR GOLDEN, COLORADO. WE SPENT SOME TIME WITH CRAIG, LAURINDA, TODD AND BECCA BLACKHAM, AND VISITING THIS FUN PARK WAS HOW WE CAPPED OFF A GREAT VACATION. THE KIDS REALLY ENJOYED THE BUMPER BOATS AND WE ALL HAD A BLAST ON THE ALPINE SLIDE! DAN, CRAIG AND LAURINDA RACED AROUND THE GO-CART TRACK! WE ATE LUNCH AT A 50'S STYLE DINER, HAD TO GET AN ICE CREAM CONE... AND SHOPPED AT THE "GENERAL STORE." WE GOT THE FUN OF AN AMUSEMENT PARK WITHOUT THE LONG LINES, AND WE SAW THE BEAUTY OF THE FOOTHILLS!

BECCA & ASHLEY ON THE ALPINE SLIDE.

BECCA, ASHLEY AND TODD DRIVING THE BUMPER BOATS.

CRAIG ZOOMS AROUND THE TRACK...

Summer of 1995-We spent a few days on Lake Mead with Devin and his family. Everyone had a great time on the boats, wave runners and the Kat, while Keith and I set up camp - Oh well.

- Eventually we got to go on the water too, while we were on the Kat it tipped over and took a piece of my thigh with it-maybe I should've stayed on the beach-or at home. It really was great to spend time with friends and play in the sun.

SWIRL

Draw it, box it, doodle it. That's all there is to these simple box letters. They're fast, they're easy, and best of all, they make you look exceedingly creative. Choose a lettering style, choose a doodle and the hard part's done.

Start with any basic lettering style such as the Roman characters shown. You can trace or draw them or use a lettering template, alphabet stickers or computer-generated lettering. Just leave enough room between each character to cut or punch them into box shapes. This style looks best when all the boxes are the same size, so be sure to center each letter in the box.

Now it's time to doodle. Thin colored pens are a great place to start, but if you prefer, branch out with geometric or textured stamps, ink splatters, watercolor swirls, little stickers, mini punches and even patterned paper backgrounds. When finished, mat each letter with multiple layers of colored and patterned paper to match your theme and colors.

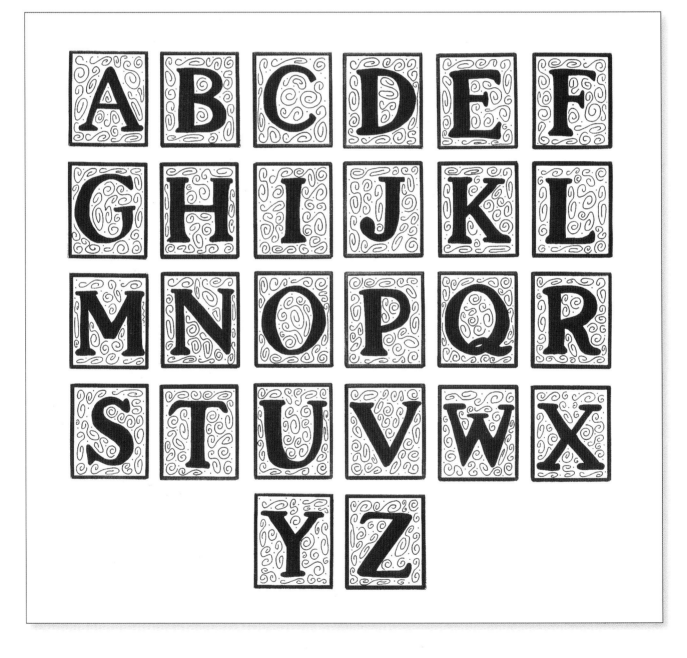

VARIATIONS

With Swirl lettering, the fun is in the doodling, so get creative and match the doodles to the theme. How about splashes for water play, stars and stripes for the good ol' USA, multicolored balls for playtime fun or curly hearts for teenage loved ones?

COLOR BLOCK

Do you like to color inside the lines, or would you rather stray outside them? If you scribble without restraint, you'll like how Color Block defines a new shape for each letter with its free-form ovals and curvy triangles and rectangles. If you are more tidy ('fess up, perfectionists), you'll be satisfied with how each vivid color neatly conforms to its defined space.

Regardless of your style, Color Block is simple to create. Start by penciling each letter with plenty of surrounding space. Because the curvy letters have few embellishments, they show up clearly against their colorful backgrounds.

Using the lettering guide for reference, pencil an oval, triangle, diamond or rectangle over the letter so that it creates different areas to color. To match the letters, keep the lines curved and deliberately imperfect.

Trace each letter with a medium to thick pen. Outline the shape with a thin pen. Now it's simply a matter of coloring each section with colored pens, pencils or the tools of choice. This time, stay inside the lines!

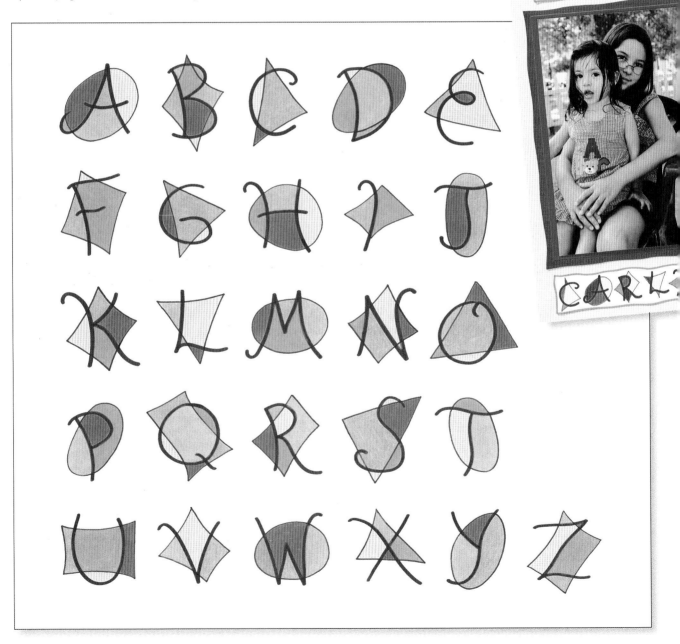

VARIATIONS

Vary the look of Color Block letters by changing the background shapes. For example, try using circles exclusively or using a shape template to draw flowers and butterflies. For added interest, use a decorative ruler to create a coordinating border.

ROMAN HOLIDAY

Quick Quiz: What do the words abacus, capital, keystone, shaft, springer and voussoir have in common? Answer: They're all parts of Roman columns and arches. Fortunately, you don't have to pass a quiz to build these letters from classic architectural elements. But you do need a little time and patience. After all, Rome wasn't built in a day!

Start by drawing pencil guidelines to keep the letter heights consistent. Then lightly pencil each character with single lines, leaving adequate space to turn each one into an architectural wonder. First transform the straight lines into columns, using a ruler to draw parallel outlines. Draw details at the column tops and bottoms (capitals and bases for you architecture buffs) and then fill in with more freeform lines to create fluted columns.

Next, transform the curved parts of each character into arches. Draw two curves to outline each arch and then fill in with short lines. Add swirls and other embellishments to complete each character.

This style looks beautiful when colored in and is ideal for special occasions such as weddings, anniversaries and proms. Use it to create an architectural statement for any page, especially those "monumental" vacations. Then, when at home, draw as the Romans!

VARIATIONS

Not just for Italian vacation pages, Roman Holiday lettering adds impact to university names, dates, official titles and more. To save time, use this style for just the first letter of a word. Also experiment with different coloring techniques such as shading with a single color or blending with two or more colors.

Millennium University

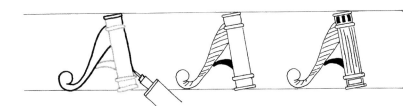

COLLEGIATE

If you ever lettered in high school or bought a sweatshirt with your alma mater's name emblazoned across the front, you'll quickly recognize this block lettering. Almost universally used for school names and athlete numbers, Collegiate is a timeless style that works equally well for vintage photos of a '50s high-school class or contemporary snapshots of youth soccer and college football.

The fastest way to re-create these letters is to trace them. First photocopy the lettering in the desired size. Starting with a guideline to keep your letters straight, trace the appropriate characters. Outline with pen, and color as desired.

You can also draw these letters using graph paper, a checker-board grid or parallel guidelines. When using graph paper, which helps keep the lines straight and the widths consistent, make sure the grid is the appropriate size. Lay a sheet of vellum or tracing paper over the grid so the lines show through. Then sketch each character using the lettering guide as a reference.

With Collegiate lettering, it's easy to show your school spirit. Dress it up with gold or silver mats for a formal graduation. Combine it with logos and mascots for college snapshots. For whimsical pages of grade school or youth sports, sketch simple stick figures and outfit them to fit the theme.

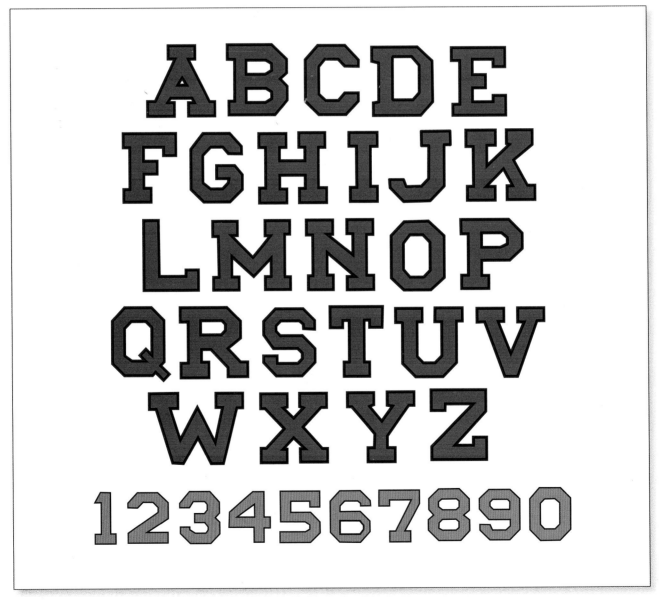

DAVID 13   ISAIAH 9   JACOB 11

VARIATIONS

Stacking a smaller word on a larger word not only keeps this Collegiate title from overwhelming the page but also adds an interesting design element. Simple stick figures provide a playful decoration, or a perfect page border, as seen on the right. Sketch each figure with a pencil, drawing a round head, triangle body and stick arms and legs. Add an outfit, shoes, hair, face and other details. Color to match your photos or theme.

WORLDWIDE

The more you travel, the more you want each travel scrapbook to be as unique as the place you visited. But you don't have to design a new lettering style each time. Simply fill in these Worldwide letters with the sights, colors, textures, patterns, themes and symbols of your destinations.

You can decorate any fill-in lettering using these ideas. To draw the Worldwide outlines, begin with two parallel guidelines the desired height of the letters. Use a ruler to sketch the straight or angled fill-in areas first. Be sure to keep the fill-in widths consistent. Then pencil in the curved lines. Add the short crossbars, or serifs, at the ends of each line or fill-in area. Trace the letter outlines with black pen.

Now comes the creative fun. Draw flag designs, animal prints and southwestern designs with colored pens and pencils. (If you have flag stickers on hand, simply cut them to fit each space.) Trim lovely shades of tropical printed paper for an Asian title. For wintry themes, stamp white snowflakes on a blue-colored background. Or just cut tiny pieces from a road map for your latest travel adventures.

VARIATIONS

Trimmed palm tree and floral stickers along with penciled details fill the Worldwide letters in this *Aloha* page. For variety, the letters were outlined with slightly squiggled lines. As illustrated by *"Our Global Adventure,"* another quick way to fill these letters is to outline them on vellum, cut out the fill-in parts and mat with patterned paper. Once you've designed your fill-in pattern, it's easy to use the same technique to design a matching border. Just draw a rectangle and fill it in.

IN BLOOM

Tulips for spring, daisies for summer, mums for fall and poinsettias for winter. Whatever the season, your titles will always be freshly blooming with these beautifully embellished letters. To grow your own, simply choose your favorite flower and unearth a calligraphy pen. Absolutely no green thumb required!

Before you begin, decide which letters to embellish, perhaps the first letter of each word or the first letter of a title or caption. Starting with penciled guidelines, sketch or trace the basic shape of each letter. For the embellished letters, sketch the flower on the left side of the character. When drawing a tulip, sketch a U shape, add a small peak at the top, and connect the peak to the sides of the U.

Color in the flower as desired. Holding a calligraphy pen at a 45-degree angle, draw the wide letter lines using separate strokes, taking care to start and stop around each flower. Complete the remaining letters and add leaves if desired. To further define each letter, highlight with a thin black pen, accenting with dots. Embellish each flower with additional details such as leaves and vines until they're blooming with color.

You Are My Sunshine

IT'S FALL AGAIN... AN[D]
PICTURES! ASHLEY IS [A]
LEE FRESHMAN. SHE [...]
ABELL JR. HIGH AT 8[...]
AT 8:40. AUSTIN IS [...]
BOWIE ELEMENTARY [...]
FROM PARKER ELEM[...]
AT 7:40. SCHOOL B[...]
THIS IS AUSTIN'S [...]

Ashley and Austin
FALL 1999

CHAPEL HILL, NORTH
CAROLINA... THE
LOCATION OF FOR
GARDEN'S SAKE, A GARDEN
CENTER AND NURSERY TUCKED
AWAY IN THE WOODS. WALTER
AND JOANN DAVIS PURCHASED
THE NURSERY IN 1999 AND
THE WORK CONTINUES AS THE
BUSINESS DEVELOPS INTO THE
AREAS OF COMMERCIAL AND
RESIDENTIAL LANDSCAPE AND
DESIGN ARCHITECTURE.

VARIATIONS

Apply the In Bloom concept to any title by incorporating a themed icon into a letter or word. Whether flowers or kites, pansies or paw prints, these embellishments add a graphic pop. If you don't want to draw, try stamps, stickers, punch art or whatever you pluck from your toolbox.

FISHBONE

If your cat were asked to design the purrfect alphabet, Fishbone, comprised of tiny fish skeletons, would be the result. You can almost imagine him licking his chops!

To draw these feline-friendly letters, first pencil the basic shape of each character with single lines. Draw triangles at the ends of the appropriate lines to represent the fish heads and tails. Refer to the lettering guide for the orientation and placement of each triangle. Erase the guidelines from inside the fish heads and tails.

Now add details. Draw the bones on each skeleton with 5 to 8 lines that vary in length. Sketch tiny black lines sprouting from the corner of the tail. Add a dot inside the fish head for the eye. When your lettering is adequately appetizing, at least to a cat, color in the triangles and trace the skeleton with a thin black pen.

Notice that letter Q and the number 2 use little fish hooks to form part of the character. Also, the number 0 is designed to look like a cat face. To sketch, narrow the bottom half of the 0 to look like a chin. Add whiskers, eyes, nose and ears. Meow!

Variations

Take the Fishbone concept and apply it to any title. Think of something that represents your page theme and incorporate it into the lettering. For example, add tiny horseshoes to a horse-themed title.

FLEAS

Oh my, Fido lost his flea collar and those pesky bugs have invaded your scrapbook. Wait, they're not real. Thank goodness, because this lettering style almost makes your skin crawl.

If you can keep from scratching, use a pencil to sketch each letter, adding the small crossbars, or serifs, wherever necessary. This lettering style is designed to feel loose and freeform, so the letters vary in size, height and width. The lines within the same character are different heights and widths and purposefully crooked. The more variety, the more whimsy.

Once you've completed each word, trace the letters with a colored pen. Next, pencil bouncing dotted lines that connect each letter. Where the lines come to a point, draw a larger dot to represent each flea. Place the dots wherever you want or follow the lettering guide for suggested placement. When you're satisfied with the design, draw over the dotted lines and flea dots with a dark pen. Now, stop that scratching!

Quinn and Allison Remund enjoy eating their food while their youngest quietly—Moments to treasure! little girl sleeps and their two-year-old sits

Ferrera Family brought friends and everyone ate lots of food—Yummy. Everyone loves a picnic! The

Memorial Day Picnic

The Evans Early's and Brasiers enjoy the picnic together and we fat the day when he got the frisbee off the roof! food to come. Far Her Abram Farty saved the

and lots of desert. The Cook family shows everyone just how much they love to eat!—Especially Lynne!*Looks good! We ate hot dogs, hamburgers, chips

VARIATIONS

Fleas lettering complements pages of perky puppies or any canine companions. To adapt this style to a completely different theme, simply change the insect. Try ants or flies for picnic pages, ladybugs and caterpillars for spring and summer themes or butterflies for flower-filled gardens.

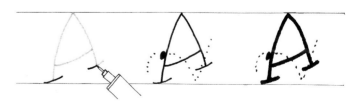

GRIN

Gimme an F! Gimme a U! Gimme an N! What's that spell? FUN! Inspired by cheerleading contortionists, these stick-figure letters add playful personality to scrapbook layouts. With a ruler and some colored pens anyone, regardless of artistic talent, can draw these animated people. Best of all, you can easily dress them up to match any occasion from A to Z.

To create your own characters, pencil top and bottom guidelines if you want the words to be straight. Using a ruler as necessary, sketch the basic shape of each letter person.

Draw the heads by tracing a small circle template or a small punched circle. The size of the circle depends upon the letter height you've chosen. Freehand draw the smaller circles for the hands or use a tiny circle template.

Trace each character with a colored pen and add faces, clothing and other accessories to match your theme. Try playground toys for summer fun, Santa hats and boots for holiday memories, angel wings and halos for your lil' darlings, bunny ears and carrots for Easter and a bride and groom for, well, you get the idea.

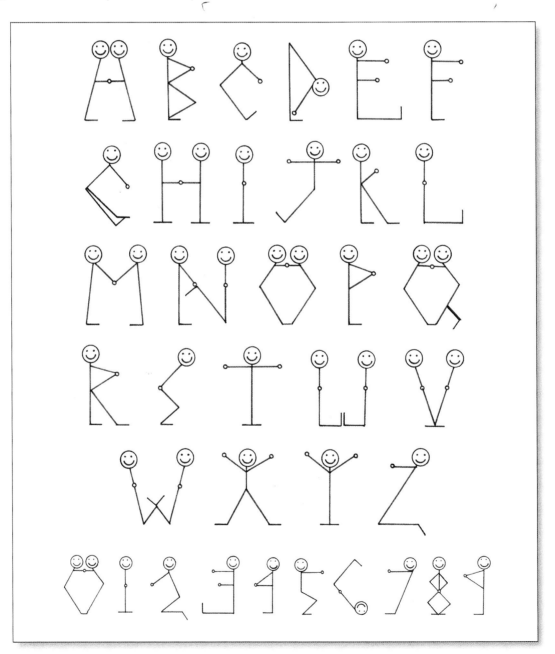

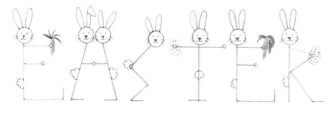

VARIATIONS

The stick people in Grin lettering can be dressed up for any occasion. Decorate all or just a few letters from your title to fit your page theme. Add a border using the same concept as illustrated by the Santa heads border. As an alternative, punch small circles for each head.

CHICKEN SCRATCH

It's fast, fun and possibly even thera-peutic. Best of all, it requires absolutely no handwriting skills. All you need to create these letters are random, reckless pen marks. This lettering is a perfect fit if you're tired of being neat and tidy.

This alphabet works well with colored pens. For a different effect try glitter or metallic pens on a dark background or bright colors on complementary papers. Combine multiple colors for even more dimension.

First lightly pencil each letter with straight lines. Notice that anywhere two lines overlap, the line extends a bit farther, as in the A, E, F, K and Y. With a fine-tip pen, scribble over the pencil lines in any fashion you choose—circles, swirls, straight lines, zigzags or jagged lines. It just doesn't get easier.

Make matching borders or try different materials such as wire, raffia or twine to create these deliberately sloppy letters. Whatever you do, have fun, and scribble away with confidence!

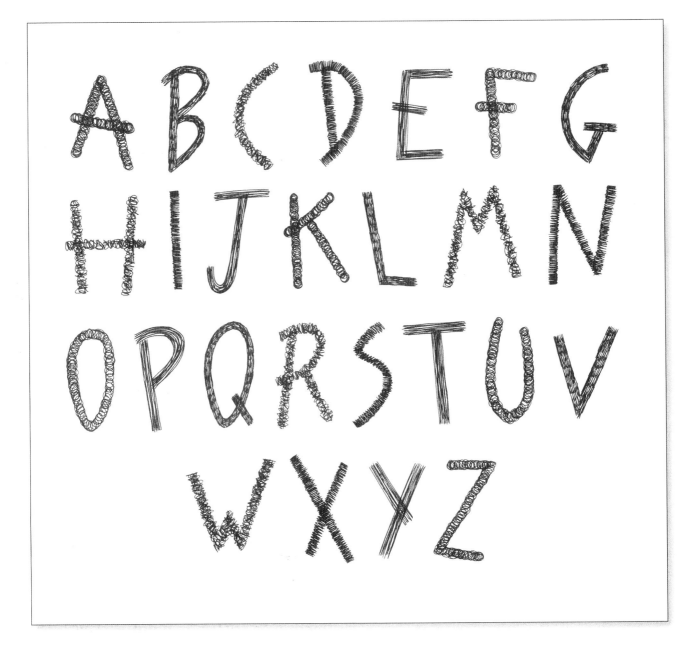

VARIATIONS

Wire letters are a natural variation for this dimensional, tactile lettering. To make the coiled letters F and L, on the *Fall* page at right, wrap thin black craft wire around a narrow rod. Then cut pieces of coil to create each line. Cut and layer various lengths of wire to create the letters A and L.

PLAYFUL

Remember the fun of Silly Putty? One popular use was to pencil a picture and press the peach-colored plastic onto it. When you removed it, the image was transferred to the Silly Putty. Now imagine doing the same thing with standard printed letters and then playing with it. Stretch the Silly Putty for the wide letters like A, E and M. Squeeze for C, D and G. And squash for the quaint O and Q. Now you have Playful lettering.

This style is particularly easy because it's a single set of all-purpose characters. The letter A, which is essentially a short fat triangle, determines the height of most letters, the width of the wide characters and the position of the middle lines in E, F and H.

Because Playful is composed of single lines, the pen size determines the weight of the letters. Use a fine-tip pen for captions but increase the pen size for titles. With the exception of O and Q, the letters line up along the same bottom and top lines. However, the casual style of this lettering invites you to raise or lower characters and extend lines above or below the guidelines. If you like, pick one element of this style that you really like, such as the long, skinny S or short and squashed O. Then incorporate that one element into your journaling to give it a playful look too.

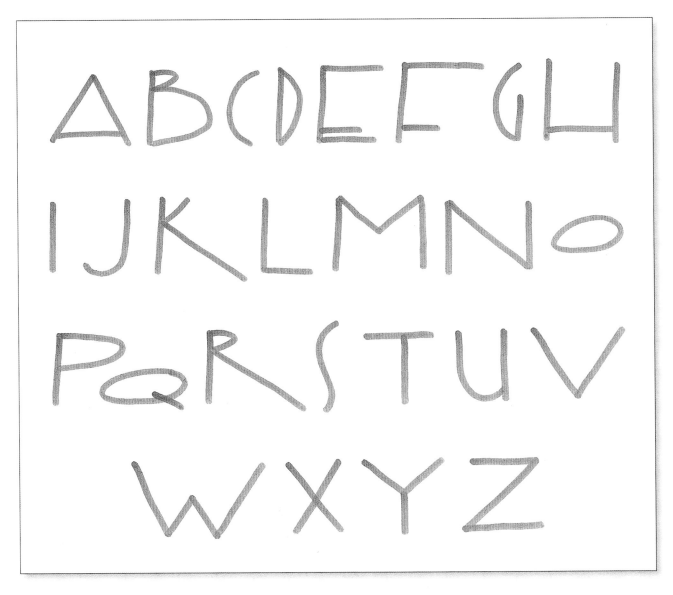

VARIATIONS

Playful can double as both a background texture and title. Its simplicity makes it easy to re-create words out of unconventional materials. The jute letters in the park page subtly suggest both the climbing ropes and the playground slide.

FUN AND FUNKY

Ever get the jaggies when you write? Maybe it's fatigue, maybe it's a bad pen, or maybe it's just that you're feeling a little rough around the edges. Whatever the reason, sometimes a title ends up looking like it's been chiseled in stone by a beginning sculptor. But this isn't necessarily bad. In fact, it's Fun and Funky.

The basic idea is to start with a fancy font and purposefully roughen every line. First pencil each character with single lines for placement. Notice that letters such as A, N and S have cute curls. Others turn into outright swirls, as in J, Y and the dramatic O. Most lines that meet also cross over, as in B, F and H. Refer to the lettering guide for the nuances of each character.

Now get jaggy on purpose. Draw around each letter with rough, crooked lines that randomly zig and zag. To finish, color in each jagged line, curl and swirl. You really cannot make a mistake, unless you're too smooth, of course.

VARIATIONS

The irregular effect of Fun and Funky lettering combines well with the crazy-quilt theme of *Guess Who?* As shown in *Yabba Dabba Doo*, a super fast way to create these rough-hewn letters is to draw them with an embossing pen and heat emboss with sparkled embossing powder. No sketching required! As an alternative to solid letters, outline them with tiny dots as in the title above, *Springtime*. Then color with pencils.

ABCDEFG
HIJKLM
NOPQRST
UVWXYZ

Yabba Dabba Doo!

"Bedrock", South Dakota
July, 1999

abcdefghijklmno
pqrstuvwxyz

0123456789
!?

GUESS WHO?

When Katie was 7, her favorite movie was "The Nightmare Before Christmas", so she dressed up as SALLY for Halloween.

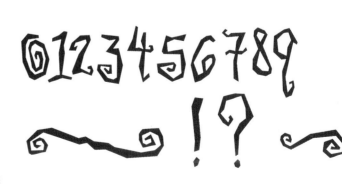

ILLUMINATED

The art of illuminated letters has its roots in the Middle Ages, when sacred manuscripts were elaborately decorated with ornate borders and illustrations. You can mimic the beauty of this craft without the painstaking labor by designing your own enlarged and embellished characters using modern tools and supplies. It might be just what you need to spice up a plain block of text.

Start by selecting the letter to illuminate. The characters shown below and on the facing page were created using the Times New Roman Bold font, but you can use any hand-drawn, stamped or computer-generated style that is simple and unadorned. Draw or print the character and cut it out. (When using letter stickers, just trim the backing paper.) Place the letter on the background and lightly trace around it to indicate the area the letter will occupy.

Lay the letter aside and decorate the background using any of the techniques listed below and illustrated on the facing page.

- Stencil the background using small stencils or embossing templates (letters A through D).
- Arrange stickers on the background to complement the theme (letters E through H).
- Trim a photo scrap to fit the letter (letters I through L).
- Use pencils and pens to embellish freehand or with a template (letters M through P).
- Stamp on the letter or background (letters Q through T).
- Use punches for the background or letter embellishments (letters U through Y).

These techniques are by no means exhaustive. You can combine them, vary them or use your own techniques for a multitude of different effects. When you're finished, simply adhere the letter to the background and incorporate the character into your title or caption.

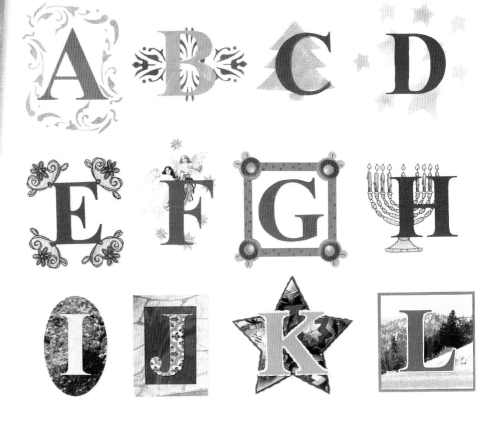

VARIATION

A single illuminated letter at the beginning of a caption or story helps draw readers into the journaling. This *Estes Park* page uses four corner designs made by matting cut-out gold leaves with printed and solid papers. One of these designs serves as the backdrop for the letter E, which is mounted with self-adhesive foam spacers to make it further stand out.

stes Park, Colorado

Jacque and I took a road trip up to Estes Park just before Christmas with our friends Amy and John. We had been there so many times in the summer months and wanted to see what life was like there during the winter. We stayed in a cozy cabin and visited the lake and the historic Stanley Hotel. One thing that stood out the most was that on this particular weekend there were fewer people and far more animals. The Elk were so close that I could almost reach out and touch one. The view of the mountains from the park took my breath away and reminded me how lucky we are to live in such a beautiful place. 2002

ADVENTURE

It's the Middle Ages, and by the light of a flickering candle, a hooded monk carefully inks a feathered quill and continues his labor of devotion—scribing highly decorative biblical texts using a writing style known as Gothic script. Fast forward 500 years, and by the light of a modern fluorescent bulb, you carefully trace these Gothic-inspired letters with an archival, pigment journaling pen to embellish your own highly decorative labor of love.

Times have changed, but classic lettering never goes out of style. This lettering makes it easy to add a classical element to pages of European travels, academic studies or any topic that evokes a sense of romance or tradition.

While you can learn to freehand these letters, unless you'll be using them frequently, it's best to just trace them using any of the methods described in the front of this book. Use a pencil to draw guidelines and outline each letter. Then trace the outlines with a dark pen and color as desired.

Traditional design elements such as fleurs-de-lis, flowers, vines, hearts and swirls combine well with Adventure lettering. Think of the types of embellishments that would appear in an old Latin Bible and you've got the picture. These letters are also ideal as decorative first letters for a title or caption. Whatever the purpose, put them to good use. After all, many monks worked hard so you could be inspired.

VARIATIONS

Gothic-inspired Adventure lettering complements these pages of European travels and academic achievement. For added emphasis, enlarge the first letter of a word and place it in a separate text block. Turn a title into a graphic element by superimposing a second word on top of the larger letters.

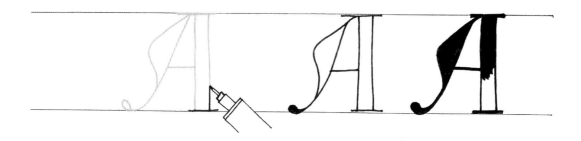

MENAGERIE

Let the fur, wrinkles, scales, fins, shells, stripes and spots creep, crawl and hop their way onto your scrapbook pages. What better way to remember trips to the zoo, nature centers, wildlife refuges or even African safaris? Not to mention pages of your favorite family pet.

Yes, it's a veritable Menagerie of interesting characters that almost leap off the page. Yet their creation is surprisingly easy. First pencil the basic letters with single lines. Use a guideline if necessary and leave plenty of space between characters. Then outline each letter with curved lines to create the smooth and rounded fill-in characters.

Now choose how to transform each character into an animal or animal part. You can copy the lettering guide exactly or simply use the designs as inspiration for your own letters. Sometimes the letter itself suggests an animal, as in the pig tail for the letter Q or the elephant trunk for the letter L. You might want to match the textures in each letter to the scales, feathers and fur of your photos. You can even cut extra animal photos into letter shapes.

Whatever your designs, make each character come alive with vivid color and texture, whether using colored pens, colored pencils, chalk, watercolors or even printed paper. When you're finished, just make sure they don't wriggle away!

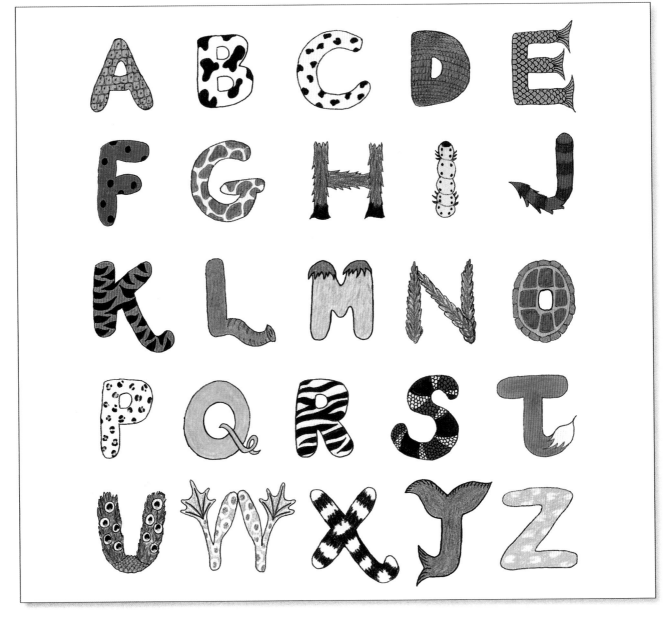

RIVERBANKS

Zoo & Botanical Garden ~ Columbia, SC

May 16, 1999 ~ It was a beautiful day for a road trip, so we headed for the Riverbanks Zoo in Columbia. The kids enjoyed seeing the animals, but the big hit of the day was definitely the Carousel. Afterwards, we went to Tony Roma's for dinner. What a perfect way to spend a gorgeous Spring day...

VARIATIONS

Menagerie lettering combines well with patterned papers and animal-theme embellishments such as the giraffe shown in *Riverbanks Zoo*. Stretch the idea even further by turning it into a frame or border idea. Wrap a striped and slithering snake around an entire layout.

NATURE CENTER

Dad took the kids to "Snakes Alive"! Courageous Chelsea & TJ petted the python!

BRANDING IRON

Round up your pony-riding, boot-stompin' and horse-shoe-slingin' snapshots 'cause it's time to lasso your western layouts with some sweetly sizzlin' letters. Inspired by cattle brands, this style is a cinch to re-create with fine-tip and chisel pens.

Start by drawing each letter with a pencil, omitting the V-shaped embellishments. Then trace each letter with a fine-tip pen. For the V shapes at the tops of the uppercase letters, hold a calligraphy or chisel pen so that its wide side is vertical relative to the baseline of the letters. Draw the V from left to right in one continuous motion—draw a short line, slope

down to touch the top of the letter, slope up and finish with another short line. Draw the V shapes at the bottom points in the same manner except upside-down.

To create the daintier embellishments on the lowercase letters, draw with only part of the pen tip so that the lines are narrower. For added decoration, shadow some or all of the letters with dashed "stitch" lines as shown on the facing page.

Complete the western theme with additional embellishments such as bandannas, cowboy hats, cowboy boots, belts, buckles, denims, plaids, leather, saddles, ropes, wagons, hay, fences...or whatever spurs your creativity.

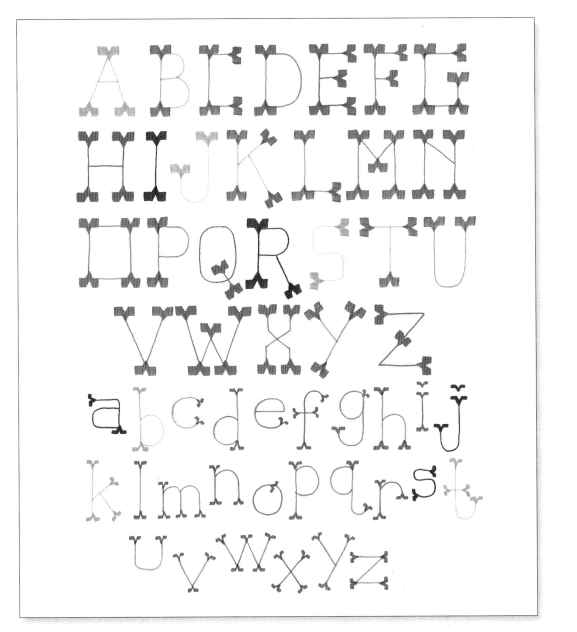

VARIATIONS

"Tie up" a western theme with a zigzag border. Use a chisel pen to draw ½" dashed lines, leaving ¼" spaces between each dash. Connect the dashes with V shapes, turning the tip so that the lines are the same width. Accent with small diamond shapes and thin dashed lines.

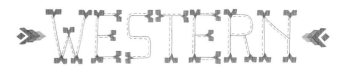

SPRING FORWARD

This lettering caters to those creative souls who love to play with color and pattern. Dots, dashes, plaids, stripes, squares, diamonds, swirls, flowers, leaves—doodle with these basic elements to fill in characters that literally "spring forward" off the page.

Starting with penciled guidelines, draw the basic shape of each letter with single lines. Next, use a ruler to transform the appropriate vertical or diagonal component of each letter into a fill-in space. Some of these spaces are rectangular boxes with straight, angled or curved ends, as in the letters F, A and J, while some have one straight side and one curved side, as in the letter C.

Follow the lettering guide to sketch each fill-in space, keeping the fill-in widths consistent. To finish each character, add the short lines, curves and swirls. When you're satisfied, color over the pencil lines with black pen.

Choose from endless combinations to fill each letter with pattern and texture. Finding inspiration in the colors, textures and theme of your layout, doodle and color to your heart's content. This lettering style is also ideal for alternative fill materials such as scraps of patterned paper, fabric, beads, buttons, eyelets, lace and ribbon. You can't have too much pattern!

VARIATIONS

Give a new "twist" to your titles using wire and sparkling beads. Form each letter and flower from thin craft wire, mount them to the page, and glue small beads inside. To protect these letters, mount a title frame with self-adhesive foam spacers.

SPRING

a b c d e f g

h i j k l m n

o p q r s t u

v w x y z

THROUGH THE AGES

Martha Cathryn
and
Joseph Elias
Wed August 12, 1894

1895

It has been said that spoken words echo only across the room, but written words echo through the ages. And so, messages left on stone tablets long ago are read today, throwing open doors to time travel. With our eyes, we understand what those who lived long ago felt in their hearts—what they feared, what they desired, what they believed. Just as telling as the scribed message is the *method* in which the missive has been set down. Throughout generations people have written down thoughts in unique ways that speak volumes about their lives. From the inception of crude prehistoric petroglyphs, through the bare, streamlined lettering style prevalent during the Great Depression, to the bright, hippie-inspired alphabet of the 60s, writing styles are both defined by, and become a symbol of the times.

PRE 1900s

What images pop to mind when you think of the Victorian Era? Antique lace, horse-drawn carriages, candlelit living rooms and quill-and-ink pen sets? Now you can capture the same old-fashioned feel with this delicate, swirling penmanship. It is easiest to replicate this lettering style by photocopying the alphabet, or tracing it using a light box. If you wish, however, to draw it freehand, begin by pencil-sketching each letter, using guidelines to assure consistent letter height. Draw the swooping letters slanting slightly to the right. Many letters, such as C, D and O, can be created without lifting your pencil from the paper, while other letters, including B and H will require two separate strokes. Strive to keep looped-shapes open, exaggerate the curled serifs and make the angles at the tops of letters such as F, H, J, K, M and N pencil-sharp. When you've finished, carefully trace over your penciled words with a fine-tipped pen. Like a perfumed hankie, this alphabet evokes ladylike charm that will weather time just like your scrapbook pages.

1900-1919

The early 1900s were a time of great change for the United States: While the country was emerging as a world leader, serious issues such as immigration, poverty, and child labor plagued the populous. World War I—the "War to End All Wars"—raged. In spite of, or perhaps because of, the turmoil, a deep-seated strength bloomed within Americans. This bold can-do, will-do attitude is evident in the shapely, defiant lettering style found in newspaper and magazine advertisements of the time. This challenging alphabet is most easily replicated by tracing. If you choose to try it freehand, note that the letters have thick vertical lines that may narrow as they enter curves, such as in C, F and G. They sit on broad bases and many have triangular serif "feet." Variations on the triangular shape appear in the mid-strokes of letters such as E and F and at the top of letters such as A, H and I. Many of these characters include curly tails that require a medium-tipped pen to draw. When creating smooth, rounded shapes, such as the letters C, D or G, try rotating your paper so you are consistently pushing, rather than pulling your pen. Add your own embellishments to make this style as homemade as apple pie.

"Ray's Return." Two simple words that say so much. The year was 1918. Ray had spent a year fighting in the trenches of Europe. I can imagine Ruth waiting on her father's farm in Sterling, Colorado without any news of her beloved. Information was hard to come by because telegrams were only sent to families who had lost a loved one. After the war had ended, Ruth would not have known when Ray would return or if he would return at all. In total, the First World War claimed eight and a half million soldiers. I picture Ruth looking out her front window waiting for Ray to walk down the dirt road. Ruth must have shouted with joy when she saw him. Someone followed her outside with a camera to photograph the kiss Ray and Ruth exchanged. They were married a few months later. This photo is very sentimental to me because Ruth and Ray were my great grandparents, and I wouldn't be here if Ray hadn't returned.

VARIATION

A bold lettering style can hold its own, even when coupled with a tiny clock, suspended charms and decorative metallic corners, or 3-D stickers. To create the *Cherished Times* title, letter on patterned paper and cover with a loosely woven web of fabric. Embellish with clock and mount on torn mulberry. Create the *Grandma's* title by lettering on mulberry paper. Double mat the title. Add sticker embellishments.

1920-1929

If there was ever an age of great prosperity in American history, the "Roaring Twenties" was it. From the great boom in consumer goods (one Model T car was produced every ten seconds) to the explosion in popular entertainment (100 million cinema tickets were sold annually), the economy seemed to be on an uphill spiral that wouldn't quit. Clearly, this tall, stylish alphabet is symbolic of a nation that was confident in its future and a bit cocky about its present. Use a medium-tip pen to draw boxy, upright letters, exaggerating the thickness, and flaring the ends of each stroke. Crossbars on most letters, including H and N, begin above the figures' waistline and are slanted upward, as though reaching for the sky. Characters such as A, R, and Y seem to be extending a foot forward, dancing the Charleston with the best of them.

ABCDEFGHIJKLMNOPQR
STUVWXYZ1234567890

CAROL STAUFFER

1930-1939

The 1930s were defined by the Great Depression, the most severe economic crises experienced by the Western world. As a result of the massive stock market crash, nearly 30 percent of Americans lost their jobs. Consumerism dropped and life was streamlined. This bare-bones lettering style, seen on many product packages at the time, reflects the austerity of the era. Create this alphabet with a ruler and a small circle template. Begin by drawing the vertical, rectangular body of the letter, using your ruler to make perfectly straight, parallel and perpendicular lines. Using the same ruler, draw in the thinner lines and then add the tiny triangles at the bottom of letters such as E, L, M and S. Use your circle template to create the curves on letters such as C, D and O. Color in hollow spaces with a medium-tipped pen. With attention to precision, your 1930s lettering will speak loudly about the unshakable fortitude of those who weathered the worst of times.

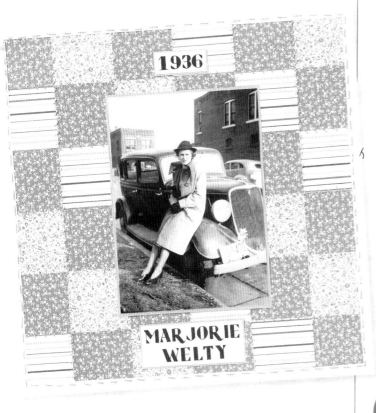

1936

MARJORIE WELTY

ABCD
EFGH
IJKL
MNO
PQRS
TUVW
XYZ
12345
67890

1940-1949

The 40s were dominated by World War II, which pulled America out of the Great Depression by reclassifying more than 50 percent of all job vacancies left by the men who were drafted. The positions were filled by women and African Americans, changing the face of America's workforce forever. The fancy script lettering so popular on consumer goods of the time speaks to the strong feminine influence that emerged as society embraced women in new careers. These free-flowing letters can be created using a fine-tip pen. Begin by penciling in the loopy forms so each sways slightly to the right. The flowing shapes end in curled serifs, and tails on letters such as G and Y are more hooked. Note that O and Q are open as are the lower loops of D and B. Make the point of having *no* points, just gentle slopes and curves, and you'll bring home the bacon for sure.

1944 & Marjorie & Susan

DECEMBER 1947

Jane 6 · Nancy 4 · David 1

1950-1959

At the end of World War II, thousands of young servicemen flocked back to the United States, eager to rebuild their shattered lives by starting new families, new jobs and new homes. With an energy never before experienced, the American economy exploded: Television sets, single-family homes and automobiles were snapped up by the thousands. A baby boom was under way. To re-create the thin-thick cursive popular during this booming period of progress, use a fine-tip pen to freehand draw letters. Add width at the top and bottom of each. While all of the letters lean slightly to the right, that's where the rule list ends. Some of the forms are open such as O and Q, some have serifs including R, T and X. M appears to melt, S is in chest-butting mode, U, V and W are only half-grown and crossbars on F and T float just above their bodies. In the post-war world in which the future was waiting to be defined, there was room to flex the muscles of individuality. This alphabet shows how it's done.

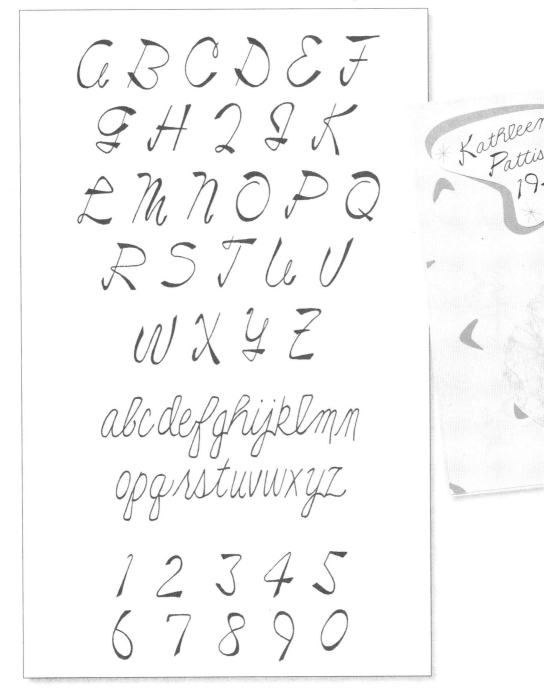

Featherstone Cty. Mn.
Family Farm 1954
Martin, Kathy, Annette,
Carol and Elinor

Bill Krum 18 yrs old
Spending a day at
Devils Lake. 1953

1960-1969

Bell-bottoms. Go-go boots. Love beads. Flowers woven into waist-length, hippy hair. With more than 76 million Baby Boomers beginning to come of age, it's no wonder the 60s—with all of their bright, boisterous fads and fashions—were dubbed "The Age of Youth." To re-create this fun, energetic alphabet, freehand draw straight line letters using a thick-tip pen. In place of serifs, draw smiley faces, peace signs, flowers or other hippie-inspired designs. For variety, use stickers, stamps or punches to embellish the letters. Don't panic if your letters are not perfectly straight. Part of this design's charm is the do-your-own-thing attitude of the individual letters. Add an extra element of funk by drawing each letter with a different color pen. Psychedelic! Peace!

1970-1979

If the 1970s were the decade of youth, the 70s were the era of *you*—as in, do your own thing. Evident by the sexual revolution, wild fashions, and pervasive, rebellious attitude of the time (ABC news anchor Sam Donaldson appeared on TV sporting long side-burns!), individuality ran rampart. This funky bubble-alphabet fits into the theme perfectly with letters that scream, "unique." While they share a few common characteristics, such as their chunkiness and ascending, graduated shading, that is where the similarities end. Want to put a pointed, curled-tailed "hook" in the middle of your I? How about leaving the curl of the O open, while making the Q appear more traditional? Who's got it? YOU!

1980-1989

The1980s, the Shop-'Til-You-Drop decade, was a period of self-fulfillment. Reach for your dream and achieve it. Let nothing stand in your way. Binge-buying, credit, designer labels, Nintendo, exercise videos, minivans and camcorders became an integral part of everyday lives. Modern technology found its toehold, influencing everything in society...including this

space-age alphabet. To create, freehand draw boxy, sans serif letters with a fine-tip pen. Add rectangular boxes to the vertical lines of each letter (with the exception of V). Then add extra rectangles just for good measure on letters such as N and R. Use the rectangular blocks to create "negative space" in letters W and M. Note that this alphabet is void of curved lines and letters such as C, D, O, P and Q are formed with right angles. Color in the thick, vertical rectangles to coordinate with your page design.

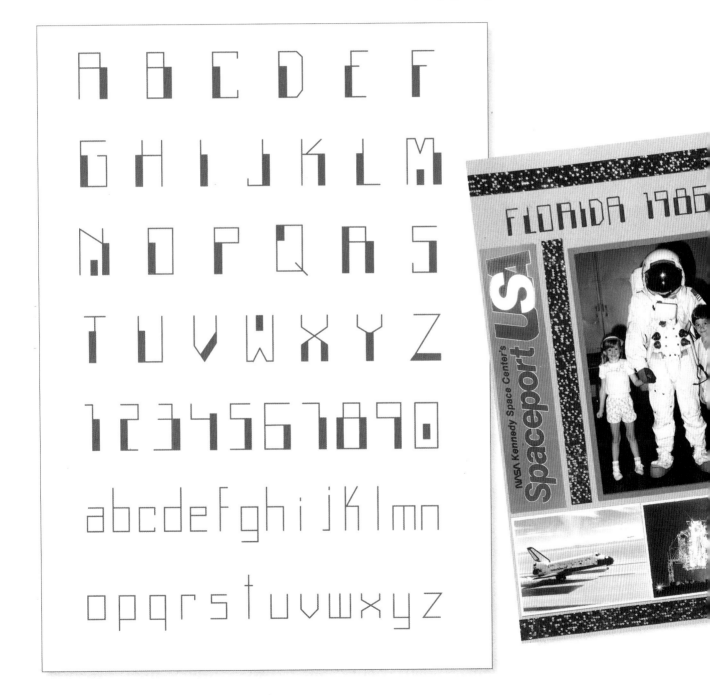

VARIATION

Freehand draw the outline of each letter. With a thick-tip black pen, color in the center space of each outlined character. Using a hole punch, remove black spaces to achieve a "Pac Man" alphabet.

1990-1999

With the birth of the World Wide Web in 1992, the 90s exploded into the electronic age, seemingly overnight. Suddenly, everything about our lives changed, from the way we communicated (e-mail), to the way we spent money (online auctions and stores), to the way we chose to do business (e-commerce). By 1998, an estimated 100 million people were online. Internet lingo like LOL (laughing out loud) and BTW (by the way) had become vocabulary standards. The computer age is reflected in the megabyte alphabet shown on the facing page. Create this techno-script using a medium tip black pen. Freehand draw thick, angular sans serif capital letters, only slightly rounding corners. With a green pen, loosely trace around the edges of each letter, extending your marks visibly beyond the edges. All green lines should be straight, even when extending across the slightly rounded portions of the black letters.

LETS EAT

CINDY AND SARAH SHARING A "MOM AND DAUGHTER" MOMENT.

JENNIFER, CAROL AND SARAH LOOK OVER THE BURGERS.

ABCDEFG
HIJKLMNOP
QRSTUV
WXYZ
1234567890

VARIATION

For a *More* playful version of this lettering style open up the letters by extending border lines around their perimeters rather than cutting into them. This creates letters with wide open fill spaces which can be easily chalked. Triple mat in primary colors and embellish the page with darling buttons.

bottomless pit

always hungry

never stops eating

Lettering Artists

Debra Beagle, Milton, Tennessee
Whimsical Block Page 36-37
Simple Stretch Page 44-45
Curved Classic Page 46-47
Debbie Davis, Spokane, Washington
Roman Holiday Page 64-65
Florence Davis, Winter Haven, Florida
Sampler/Inspired Page 24-25
Cindy Edwards, Highland, Michigan
Chicken Scratch/Inspired Page 78-79
Sarah Fishburn, Fort Collins, Colorado
Contempo Page 32-33
Pamela Frye, Denver, Colorado
Fun and Funky Page 82-83
Mary Conley Holladay, Jacksonville, Florida
Hearts Entwined Page 56-57
Lisa Jackson, San Antonio, Texas
Juliann Page 38-39
Fishbone Page 72-73
Fleas Page 74-75
Jan March, Hilton, Iowa
1980s/Pac Man Page 107
Lindsay Ostrum, Colfax, California
Shaker Page 26-27
1980s Pac Man/Inspiration Page 107
Allison Pavelek, Salem, Oregon
Adventure/Inspired Page 86-87
Michelle Pesce, Arvada, Colorado
Slant Page 28-29
Elegance Page 34-35
Charity Ball Page 40-41
Grace Page 48-49
Worldwide Page 68-69
Narda Poe, Midland, Texas
Architecture Page 42-43
Holly Page 52-53
Sunburst Page 58-59
Swirl Page 60-61
In Bloom Page 70-71
Playful Page 80-81
Tammy Prueitt, Westminster, Colorado
Bow Tie Page 14-15
Carol Snyder, Alpine, Utah
Branding Iron Page 90-91
Emily Tucker, Matthews, North Carolina
Puttin' On The Ritz/Inspiration Page 50-51
Menagerie Page 88-89
JoAngela Vassey, Cherry HIll, New Jersey
Grin Page 76-77
Sande Womack, Littleton, Colorado
Fluffy Page 16-17
Elementary Page 18-19

Signature Page 20-21
Pinstripe Page 22-23
All For One Page 30-31

Memory Makers Lettering By

Pamela Frye
Erikia Ghumm
Pam Klassen
Sampler Page 24
Puttin' On the Ritz Page 50-51
Cross Stitch Page 54-55
Color Block Page 62-63
Collegiate Page 66-67
Worldwide/Inspiration 68-69
Chicken Scratch Page 78-79
Illuminated Page 84-85
Spring Forward Page 92-93
Thru The Ages Lettering Pages 94-109
(except 1980s/Pac Man)

Art

Art that appears in this book and is not credited on these pages was created by *Memory Makers* artists.

Page 14 *Bow Tie*
Border/Inspiration
By Jodie Bushman Welches, Oregon

Page 16 –17 *Fluffy*
Coincidental Cousins, Mom and Perry Como & Debbie and Sande
By Sande Womack Littleton, Colorado

Page 18-19 *Elementary*
Young Ameritowne
By Sande Womack Littleton, Colorado
Titles
By Brandi Ginn 2003 MM Master, Lafayette, Colorado

Page 20-21 *Signature*
When in Rome & Falling for Fall
By Sande Womack Littleton, Colorado

Page 22-23 *Pinstripe*
China Business Trip, Annual Christmas Card, They Say It's Your Birthday, Unwrap Smiles
By Sande Womack Littleton, Colorado

Page 24-25 *Sampler*
A Mother's Love & Titles
By Brandi Ginn 2003 MM Master, Lafayette, Colorado

Page 26-27 *Shaker*
Hangin' Out With Miss Jeannie, Out of Our Gourd & Titles
By Lindsay Ostrum Colfax, California

Page 28-29 *Slant*
Christmastime
By Michelle Pesce Arvada, Colorado
My Girls
By Brandi Ginn 2003 MM Master, Lafayette, Colorado

Page 30-31 *All For One*
Hemet High, Lucy Lu Bigglesworth & Columbine Wildcats
By Sande Womack Littleton, Colorado

Page 32-33 *Contempo*
Titles
By Brandi Ginn 2003 MM Master, Lafayette, Colorado
(Photos by Lorna Dee Christensen, Covallis, Oregon)

Page 34-35 *Elegance*
Spring, Honour of Your Presence & Titles
Michelle Pesce Arvada, Colorado
Page 36-37 Whimsical Block
Nuts Over Acorns, Jet Skiing Fun & Fire Chief
By Debra Beagle Milton, Tennessee

Page 38-39 *Juliann*
Laura's Graduation & My New Ornament
By Lisa Jackson San Antonio, Texas
Titles
By Brandi Ginn 2003 MM Master, Lafayette, Colorado

Page 40-41 *Charity Ball*
Faces of Tigger, Auntie's Shower & Titles
By Michelle Pesce Arvada, Colorado

Page 42-43 *Architecture*
Little Shaver, Wild Blue Yonder & Vacation
By Narda Poe Midland, Texas

Page 44-45 *Simple Stretch*
Ballet Class, Artist Eggs-traodinaire & The Huntress
By Debra Beagle Milton, Tennessee

Page 46-47 *Curved Classic*
Mi Abuela & Reading Rocks
By Debra Beagle Milton, Tennessee

Page 48-49 *Grace*
Dunsmuir House & Titles
By Michelle Pesce Arvada, Colorado

Index